CW00766270

MR. Z

By: Don Zarin

Copyright © 2022 by Don Zarin

All rights reserved

First published in 2024

No part of this book may be used or reproduced in any matter whatsoever without written permission except in the case of brief quotations embodied in critical articles and reviews. For information, write to: MrZbook.com

Library of Congress Cataloging-in-Publication Data
Name: Zarin, Don, author
Title: Mr. Z
Identifiers: Library of Congress Control Number: 2024906270 /ISBN 979-8-9901659-0-8 (hardcover)/ISBN 979-8-9901659-1-5 (paperback)/ISBN 979-8-9901659-2-2 (ebook)
Subjects: LCSH: Gambling|Compulsive gamblers
BISAC: Games and Activities/Gambling
(See also Self-Help/compulsive behavior/gambling)

This true story is a work of creative nonfiction. The events are based on thousands of pages of depositions and testimony from the extensive litigation and ensuing investigations; thousands of pages of legal and project documents; casino records; interviews with more than a dozen key persons still alive today; and numer-ous newspaper articles published during the relevant time period. Some of the dialogues are direct quotations; in other cases, I reconstructed conversations based on my memories and the recollections of others who participated in or witnessed these interactions. I also relied on literary creativity to imagine conver-sations and meetings that I believe likely took place, based on my knowledge of the individuals involved and their interactions with each other. In a few instances, I speculated on what may have happened to fill in gaps in the narrative.

Printed in the United States

Contents

ACKNOWLEDGEMENTS

I would like to acknowledge the many people who encouraged, assisted and supported me in the writing of this book. First and foremost, I want to thank my wife, Bobby. She participated actively in the many interviews I conducted in researching this story. She edited the manuscript throughout the process, and encouraged me to continue. She listened to the story as it developed, and gave me very helpful commentary to improve the telling of the story. My brother-in-law, Charles Crawford, brought his literary knowledge and editing skills to each chapter, and made important and substantive improvements. My daughter. Leslie Schreibman, and my friend, Joel Zipp, read and diligently edited each chapter as I proceeded. My thanks also to Suzanne McGee and Susan Rivers of Singular Stories for helping me develop my manuscript into a finished book. I also wish to thank my agent, Claudia Menza, for her unstinting support. Many people generously gave their time and agreed to be interviewed, sometimes for a long period of time. I couldn't have told this story without their help.

Finally, some people have asked me why I wrote this book, and whether it was for cathartic reasons. The answer is that I wrote this book because I thought it was a remarkable true story that needed to be told.

PROLOGUE

March 15, 1980

It's his best night ever.

"Mr. Z", the highest roller in craps at Atlantic City's Resorts International Casino is on a winning streak. At his fingertips lie rows of green $500 chips and black $100 chips, the proceeds of 20 rolls of the dice. He absently smooths his rumpled tie, squares his shoulders and prepares to toss number 21. He surveys his chips totaling $22,500 spread across the table, a combination of bets that would be worth over $87,800 today. If he rolls a 7, he loses it all.

A dark-haired woman in a pink Chanel shift leans slightly forward over the table edge. He grins at her and picks up two dice between his thumb and index finger, making sure the number 4 is facing up. Extending his hand in her direction, "Blow on the dice," he tells her, suggestively. Other players around the table exchange glances. She leans toward him, their bodies touching. She blows softly, meets his eyes, and winks.

Turning his body sideways, he flings the dice into the air over his head. They bounce once, twice and then against the rubber bumper on the opposite end of the table.

"Six!" cries the stickman. The table erupts in cheers.

Another win for "Mr. Z".

The knots of spectators, four rows deep around the table, clap as the croupier rakes in the dice; the dealer slides the winnings to Mr. Z, as David Zarin is known to everyone in Atlantic City.

Dave has been standing at the craps table for 13 hours, taking only short breaks to grab some food or hit the restroom. Now, a waitress in a short red cocktail dress slips a fresh martini onto the small shelf beneath the table edge, and deftly whisks away an older drink, untouched. He doesn't notice. His dilated dark brown eyes are riveted to the table's numbered green felt. He signals to the dealer to add some of his winnings to his other bets. A few fellow players follow his lead, hoping to hitch a ride on his hot streak. The stickman pushes the dice back to Dave. He again sets them so the number four is face up. The crowd applauds, chanting "Mr. Z! Mr. Z!". Even the casino waiters and security guards stop and crane their necks over the crowd to watch. Dave tightens his jaw. His eyes are fixed only on his chips. All business, he tosses again.

"Eight!" yells the stickman, with uncharacteristic excitement. Even when he worked Vegas, he's never seen such a bold player.

David Zarin cuts a handsome figure at six feet tall with curly salt-and-pepper hair; but it's his magnetic personality and aggressive gambling style that always draws a crowd to his table. The bigger the crowds, the bigger the profits for the casino. So, Resorts owners and managers work hard to keep him coming back, plying him with free rooms, food, drinks, and other perks. At this time he's the biggest gambler on a sustained basis anywhere in the world.

Flushed, sweating and euphoric, Dave punches the air, soaking up the attention and excitement of the crowd. The woman in pink is beaming and stroking his shoulder. He's never felt more alive.

"Craps", he says, "is better than sex."

***

But Dave Zarin has another side. A successful real estate developer, he has parlayed his business savvy and appetite for risk into successfully developing affordable housing in Pennsylvania, Florida, and now, Atlantic City. As state officials hail legalized casino gambling as the cure for the storied resort's dying economy, Dave is the one developer willing to gamble on that revival by building affordable housing.

Mr. Z was my dad. He was a consummate risk-taker, gregarious and exciting to be around. All the qualities that made him a successful entrepreneur. Yet, looking back, I see how that love of risk devolved into a gambling addiction and turned our whole family's life upside down. For a long time, no one in our family – not even Dave himself – realized he was out of control. Years later, a detailed account of his exploits – and their stunning cost – would fill thousands of pages of court documents. But we'll get to that later.

Even if we had understood his addiction, I doubt Dave's story would have unfolded differently. His story is really *our* story: about our family and the many people who knew and admired him, in all his complexity. He was mercurial, yet charming. Fearless at work and in the casino. But Dave also was a compassionate and politically astute businessman who recognized that bringing affordable housing to Atlantic City was critical to fueling its economic comeback and to improving the lives of its residents. He spotted what other developers missed: a potential source of growth and profit that would benefit all the city's citizens.

Through it all, until his death in 2005, and to this day, I consider my dad to have been one of my best friends. Despite all that our family endured because of his compulsion I still love and accept him as he was.

CHAPTER 1: THE STARTING GATE

When he isn't taking some kind of risk, Dave feels like he's living in a 1950s black and white film. Like millions of other American men in the postwar era, he's busy working and raising a family. When he makes bets in business or at the casino, however, it's as if someone flips a switch and his world bursts into technicolor. The thrill of gambling – whether on a business deal or at a craps table – isn't really about the money for Dave. It's about the exhilarating roller coaster of adrenaline: the climbing anticipation and anxiety, reaching a crest before the inevitable plunge into a steep drop, win or lose. In craps, a growing pile of chips proves a gambler's skill; the bigger the risks the greater the guts. Dave is proud that he has plenty of both.

The son of striving, middle class Russian immigrants, Dave has come a long way from his modest childhood in Newark, New Jersey. As a tall, wiry and athletic youth at Weequahic High School, he's a standout on the basketball court as team captain. His high school sweetheart, Louise Knapp, was born to Hungarian immigrants; the pretty, petite blonde is as reserved and quiet as Dave is self-assured and gregarious. They met in junior high school.

Louise's parents run a modest diner in Manhattan at the mouth of the Holland Tunnel near Canal Street. Louise is a good student, but her family can't afford to send her to college, so she instead trains as a dental assistant.

Because of the Knapps' blue-collar background, my father's mother disapproves of the match between Dave and Louise. Nevertheless, they marry soon after my father finishes college in 1939, on the eve of the outbreak of World War II. My father can't afford an engagement ring, but that doesn't matter to Louise. She "only had eyes for him," she tells us years later, somewhat wistfully.

Dave earns a degree in civil engineering from the Newark College of Engineering. During the war years, as his peers set off for the front lines in Europe and the Pacific, Dave is assigned a job as a naval architect at Philadelphia's Navy Yard. Far from the excitement of combat, he chafes at the tedium of his daily grind. But when he picks up poker to break the monotony, he discovers the thrill of winning and losing, the highs and the lows, even when the stakes are tiny.

After the war, Dave and Louise seem to settle down to ordinary life. Dave builds up a civil engineering business while Louise devotes her life to building a home for him and their growing family. Eventually, they have three children, each born about five years apart – two sons, my older brother Richard, then me, and finally my sister, Robin. In 1950, we move into a modest suburban two-story house in Elizabeth, N.J. The living room's highlight is a large picture window overlooking the quiet tree-lined street. The house has a small kitchen, three small bedrooms and a single bathroom. Louise keeps the yellow upholstery of our living room sofa pristine, covering it with plastic slipcovers that feel sticky and make shrill creaking sounds when we sit on them. This furniture shares space with a baby grand piano that once belonged to my father's parents. Our family will live in that house for more than 25 years.

I remember my youth as idyllic, a *Leave it to Beaver* universe: My father is the bread winner; Louise is the quintessential homemaker. She runs the household and takes care of the children. She makes a point of always being home when we kids return from school. She wants to make us feel secure. She's an accomplished cook and *de facto* den mother to our friends, regularly baking treats for the neighborhood kids. We play football in the street and ride bikes through the neighborhood. All of our friends seem to end up hanging out at our house; Louise is the most popular mom on the block.

She's the family anchor and Dave counts on her to provide a steady and predictable home life. In contrast, his burgeoning engineering and real estate development ventures are a constant gamble. The projects he backs have about as much chance of failing as they do of succeeding.

Many small business entrepreneurs operate their business with one foot on the cliff and one foot dangling off its edge. They radiate confidence even as they're only a single step away from failure. In my father's case, a five-foot board extends out from that cliff edge. He's often clinging to that board, dangling from it by two or three fingers. If others take risks, Dave's are especially bold. He thrives on risk. He never doubts his own savvy both in business and gambling.

In addition to taking chances in his business, Dave develops a passion for bridge. He becomes a Life Master in the card game, qualifying him to play at the illustrious Cavendish Club in Manhattan. This exclusive club, which limits its membership to 400, hosts the world's top bridge players. Reflecting the status of those players, the money stakes at the Cavendish Club are very high, so Dave studies bridge strategies ferociously. He becomes so skilled at the game that he can hold his own against celebrity masters like movie star Omar Sharif and Charles Goren, the author of best-selling books about the game. A consummate networker, Dave frequently chauffeurs Goren to deliver speeches or play in tournaments so they can discuss the nuances of bidding in bridge. My father approaches bridge as he does most of his endeavors – with an intense drive to learn and excel.

He taught me the game at an early age. When I was about 13 years old, I began playing in duplicate bridge tournaments with my father. In duplicate bridge, a team of two players (a "pair") plays the same arrangement of cards as other bridge pairs, with final scores calculated by comparing each pair's result with others who played the same hand. Generally, each pair plays 24 hands during the tournament. After the tournament, my father, who has a remarkable memory and ability to concentrate, can recall the play in each of the 24 games, and can accurately describe the cards each player held, an astounding feat. Unfortunately, I never become very good, much less come close to matching my father's skill. My mother is a good bridge player but refuses to play duplicate bridge with my father. It's often said that bridge couples who play together don't stay together. The arguments between married partners can be particularly intense.

In Dave's postwar poker games, the stakes are exponentially higher than those he played for in his days at the Navy Yard. In New York, he hangs out at the poker table with well-known television and film actors and writers. One of the most memorable personalities is film and TV writer Jerry

Marvin, a tall thin man with a mustache and big personality and a laugh to match. Known as a "gambler's gambler," Jerry can charm a snake. He and my father wager on anything, for all kinds of stakes: $1,000, the expenses for a trip to Vegas, or simply dinner. Dave loves rubbing elbows with the rich and famous, including film director Mike Nichols and Ivan Reitman. Even playing with a faster crowd and placing bigger bets, Dave holds his own. In one game, he wins a large sum from a well-known Hollywood producer. In the era before ATM machines, the out-of-towner didn't have enough cash with him to cover his loss. So he goes into the men's room, tears off a piece of toilet paper and writes out a "check" for $20,000. He hands it to Dave, who later successfully deposits the strip of tissue at his bank.

The ups and downs of Dave's business mirror his gambling wins and losses. He's either flush with cash or flat broke. In theory, Dave gives my mother money for the household expenses each week. In reality, it's hit or miss, depending on whether he's winning or losing. Sometimes after a big gambling win, Dave will give Louise some extra cash, only to end up asking for it back after a big loss. Louise, always frugal and responsible, copes with the uncertainty by asking her older sister, Alice, who lives only a few miles away, to keep a cache of money for her. Louise is adept at the financial juggling act that Dave's risk-taking requires, but even so she's sometimes short of money to pay the bills; and borrows from Alice to tide them over until Dave's next big win.

Throughout these ups and downs, it weighs on Dave that alone among her friends, Louise doesn't have an engagement ring. So, in 1969, after one of his biggest wins, he resolves to make it up to her. Coming home one evening, he waves a wad of cash in front of her.

"Louise, I always wanted to give you an engagement diamond," he says. "Take this and buy yourself anything you like."

Louise gasps as she watches him count out $15,000 in bills and drop them in her hand. Remember, this is the late 1960s and that sum is enough to buy a serious piece of jewelry. Louise chooses an impressive four carat pear-shaped diamond with one large baguette on each side, a popular style at the time. More than once, I catch her gazing in wonder at her ring.

As I grow up, I join my dad on many of his outings and gambling jaunts. Once or twice a month, Dave takes me along on his weekly visit to the Turkish-Russian baths, inevitably followed by a trip to the race track. These nights out make up some of my happiest and most vivid memories of bonding with my dad. Typically, Dave meets my grandfather Meyer and my Uncle Ira every Thursday at the *schvitz*, either Silver's Baths on Coney Island or at Luxor Baths in the heart of New York's theatre district. Wrapped in white sheets, we sit on large wooden chairs in the sauna room, sweating and talking as attendants bring us cups of water and place cool wet towels on our heads.

Jon Epstein, my closest buddy (who lives across the street) sometimes joins us. But my older brother Rich prefers to hang out with his friends at home. The Luxor Baths are in a nine-story building and evoke a bygone era with a prominent sign that reads "For Men Only." The main entrance resembles a hotel lobby. You place your wallet, watch, and other valuables in a safety deposit box. The clerk locks them up behind the check-in desk, then hands you a key on an elastic band that you wear around your wrist during your stay. The clerk assigns each guest his own locker and a bed on a dormitory floor, and hands him a white cotton sheet, towel, and canvas slippers.

The main floor has a large sauna room, a scented steam room and the "Russian room", all arranged around a central ice-cold pool. Off to the side are a row of massage tables. My father and uncle sit together in the sauna room and exchange "war" stories. My father's tales all involve real estate projects constantly teetering between success and failure; Uncle Ira spins one yarn after another about his representation of injured plaintiffs in personal injury lawsuits. I sit close to them and listen, fascinated. The Russian room, my favorite, has three wooden benches set at different levels. Periodically, someone throws water on the hot rocks in an oven. The steam coming off the rocks quickly heats the room to a high temperature. I love to fill wooden buckets with ice cold water from a water spout and pour it over myself to keep cool.

After the sauna baths, we stop at a nearby restaurant for dinner. Sometimes it's our favorite Jewish deli, where my grandfather eats slabs of salami and French fries. On other occasions, we go to a steak restaurant, where each of the men devours large T-bones. But before long, Dave just skips the dinner with his father and brother, heading instead to Yonkers Racetrack or Roosevelt Raceway to watch harness racing. I love those weeknight outings, even if I do have a hard time getting up for school the next day.

I'm about eight years old when my dad buys box seats for the season at Monmouth Racetrack in Long Branch, N.J. Watching and wagering on the thoroughbred horse races becomes a family outing every Saturday. However, our day out doesn't end with the last race at Monmouth. Dave prolongs the excitement by taking us to

Yonkers Raceway or Roosevelt Racetrack on Long Island to watch the nighttime harness races. My father and I both relish the excitement of the track; together, we pore over the racing form and discuss the details of each race, the horses' lineage, past races and winnings. Dave even makes small bets for me and lets me keep any of my modest winnings. My mother and my sister Robin dutifully come along, but bring magazines or crossword puzzles to pass the time. "This is what I call family together-ness," my father declares heartily, prompting surreptitious eye rolls from Louise and Robin. My older brother Rich almost never joins us. By now he's a teenager and has his own friends and interests; soon, he leaves home to attend Rutgers University.

Despite the cyclical ups and downs of the commercial construction industry, Dave is building his engineering business into a successful enterprise. To broaden the company's scope by allowing it to both design and build projects, Dave hires an architect. He decides to focus on constructing nursing homes, a nascent but promising market niche. In 1962, he designs his first nursing home in Parsippany, N.J., for a client who couldn't get financing for the venture. When the client's project is on the verge of cratering, Dave decides to raise the money himself, considering it too great an opportunity to miss. His geniality, command of details and charisma make Dave a great salesman and he convinces a lawyer friend in Los Angeles, John Fernbach, to help him identify backers. Together, John and Dave persuade a number of Hollywood actors, producers and writers to invest in the venture, including comedian Jonathan Winters, 1930s film star Sylvia Sydney and the actress and TV game show panelist Arlene Francis.

The success of this first nursing home project launches him into real estate development. Always astute when it comes to calculating the odds, Dave realizes that there's a way to do something good and to make a profit at the same time. He anticipates that an aging population and changing demographics will fuel demand for nursing home facilities. Long before many of his peers recognize that trend, Dave already has begun to build and sell nursing homes in New Jersey and Pennsylvania.

But developing nursing homes is a long and complex process. There's a good chance that something will go wrong: The financing might fall through, or Dave might not get the regulatory approvals and permits he needs. If a project fails, Dave will often have to repay the monies that investors have advanced to cover the pre-construction expenses and the costs of running his office.

The result? Dave is continually trying to keep pace on an ever speeding treadmill. To cover his overhead – to pay investors, to keep his business running and to maintain his gambling lifestyle – he always needs to identify more and more projects and to have a greater percentage of these succeed. As his business becomes more complex and as he gambles more heavily, Dave and Louise begin to argue more often. He wants a wife who can follow his thoughts when he talks about the intricacies of the deals he's putting together; a partner who grasps the nature of the problems he confronts. When Dave first opened his business, and until Rich was born, Louise had helped out in the office by handling administrative and clerical tasks. But when Rich comes along, she instead focuses on her role as mother and homemaker and isn't particularly interested in the company. As a result, Louise isn't aware of how much pressure Dave's under from the risks he is taking.

He begins to berate her, and does so with increasing frequency. Often, he picks on something irrelevant or meaningless as a proxy for his general frustration. Louise serves chicken too often; Louise wants to head home early from a dinner party. If she comments on any business matter, he belittles her. "What the hell do you know?" he growls. Abhorring confrontation, Louise falls silent. She simply endures his verbal abuse.

One of the worst of these confrontations takes place when I am about 11 years old. I'm doing my homework at the dining table while my mother is fixing dinner. When my father comes home, my mother hurries to the front door to welcome him. Even from my chair I can see Dave's face; I can tell he's in a dark mood. I can't make out their conversation at first, they speak so quietly. But within minutes my father's voice escalates and he's shouting.

"You really don't get it, Louise! You're really stupid. It's hopeless trying to explain anything to you," he yells.

Dave keeps berating her so loudly that my brother Rich hears him bellowing from our bedroom. He rushes downstairs. At the age of 16, he's now almost as tall as Dave. He steps in between my father and mother.

"STOP yelling at Mom!" Rich screams, directly into Dave's face. "Quit pushing her around! We all have to live with your abuse and I'm sick and tired of it."

My father steps back, shocked into silence. His face reddens in fury and he clenches his fists. By now I've bolted from the dining room to see Rich and my father face each other, both of them rigid with anger.

"It's not fair," Rich adds. "Especially to Mom. Just cut it out."

When my brother finishes his rant, my father – still stunned – relaxes his hands and lets out a loud sigh. "I'm going out for a drive," he mumbles. Flinging open the front door, he signals to me to join him. I follow without saying a word.

We drive around the neighborhood in silence for what feels like an eternity. Suddenly, Dave asks a question that shakes me to my core. "How would you feel if your mother and I got divorced?"

Speechless, I burst into tears. My mind's racing: What will happen to us? What will my mother do? Where would we live? After about a minute, Dave pulls the car over to the side of the road. He reaches over and grabs my hands. "Don't worry, that will never happen," he says, putting his arm around my shoulders and giving me a firm squeeze. I believe him and my sobbing trails off into sniffles. As with the other blowups between my parents, the conflict ends fairly quickly and relative calm seems to return to our house. But as I will later realize, the relationship between Rich and my father will never be the same again.

It's inevitable that Dave discovers the excitement and intensity of Las Vegas. He begins visiting casinos there once or twice a year. When I'm 13, I accompany him on one of his trips and notice that all the casino employees seem to know him and even to know who I am. He, in his turn, greets several of them by name and even asks how their families are doing.

"How well you treat people who have no power over you says a lot about you," he explains to me.

This proves to be his last trip for a while. He loses $50,000 (equivalent to $470,000 today) at craps and the casino cuts off his credit. In spite of those losses, he leaves generous tips for the dealers, staff and servers. He eventually pays off the debt, though it takes him three years to do so.

In the mid-1960s, when I'm about 15 years old, my parents buy a two-bedroom vacation condominium overlooking the beach in Hallandale, Florida. The city happens to be the home of several major U.S. horse racing tracks. During one holiday in the condo, Dave looks up from the Daily Racing Form he's reading and points out an ad announcing a horse auction for two-year-old thoroughbreds in training for racing. It's taking place at a horse breeding farm about an hour's drive away. "It might be fun to take a look," Dave suggests, with a gleam in his eye. It sounds interesting and novel, so I drop my plan to hit the beach and join him for another Dave Zarin adventure.

The farm is every bit as picturesque as I had imagined. Horses graze in the sunny pastures that line the long driveway; greenery and rustic wood fences border each field. At the end of the drive stands a big blue barn and an imposing white-columned stone house. Dave grabs a catalogue describing the 15 horses to be sold that day and joins the group of potential buyers gathering in front of the auctioneer's podium. A groom leads the first horse into a roped-off area, a muscular but still lean two-year-old colt with a gleaming black coat and while strip on his face. The auctioneer recites details of its breeding and its training. The potential buyers appear more nervous than the thoroughbred whose fate is in their hands. The auctioneer breaks into a rapid-fire sing-song chant; potential buyers vie with each other to place their bids. The final price for that horse is (to me) a whopping sum: $65,000.

Dave watches the auctioneer sell three more horses. By the time the fifth horse appears, I'm bored and ready to leave. Then my dad shoots his hand into the air.

My mouth drops.

"Did you just bid on that horse?"

My dad grins.

"It might be fun to own a racehorse," he says.

Dave buys two horses that day. And so, begins his obsession with thoroughbred horse racing.

Dave ships the horses to a trainer at Monmouth Park. Later, he adds several more thoroughbreds to his stable and races them at tracks up and down the East Coast. Thanks to my father's foray into horseracing, I come to know a lot about the sport and how to handicap thoroughbreds using the Daily Racing Form.

About a year later, my father's trainer, Buddy, calls to tell him to go to Monmouth that afternoon. One of Dave's horses is running in a race he can't lose. Buddy always struck me as a shifty character and later incidents confirm it. In this case, he had deliberately held the horse back from winning in its previous race and has now entered the horse in a race against far less qualified horses. It's a common ploy in horseracing and sets up as good a bet as you can have without a fix. I play hooky from high school and head out to the track with my dad. My grandfather Meyer, now in his mid-eighties, lives nearby and enjoys visiting the track to watch the horses. That day he joins us, pushing his walker with those bright yellow tennis balls on its feet. Unlike Dave, he rarely bets more than two dollars on a race. Our horse, in the sixth race, is number 5. As the horses approach the track, we all leave our seats to place our bets. Despite his age, my grandfather is pretty spry with the walker; he expertly steers himself to the betting window and back again. As the horses line up at the starting gate, he settles himself heavily into his seat. He's got a half-smile on his lips, as if he's just heard a private joke. When our horse wins easily, by six lengths. I'm jumping up and down with excitement. Then I notice my grandfather crumpled in his seat, and wearing a look of surprise and disappointment. I frown.

"Grandpa, what's the matter? Didn't you bet on our horse?"

Reddening in embarrassment, he looks at me sheepishly.

"When I was peeing in the bathroom, the guy in the urinal next to me leaned over and gave me a tip on another horse," he confesses. "I bet on *his* tip."

Dave's finest horse, named Robdale after my sister, Robin Dale Zarin, has been winning, or placing second or third, in a number of impressive races. My dad is obsessed with this colt. Then comes a race on a rain-drenched track. Buddy has previously assured Dave that Robdale is a "mudder," meaning that he runs well on a muddy track. On our way to the track in the car, Dave keeps saying, "It's raining, it's raining. Robdale's a mudder. He's a mudder. This is going to be a great day."

Arriving at the track Dave heads straight for Buddy.

"The horse is going to win, isn't he?" he asks the trainer anxiously. "He's a mudder. It'll be great, won't it?"

Buddy looks away and shrugs. "I dunno. He's a horse. We'll see how he does."

Robdale doesn't win that day. Neither does Dave.

In 1972, Dave and Buddy enter Robdale in a big-stakes race, a run-up to the Kentucky Derby, at Garden State Racetrack in Cherry Hill, N.J. He's a medium-to-long shot among the three-year-olds competing that day. Out of the gate, he's dead last. The race plays out like a scene in a classic movie. The announcer's nasal voice booms over the loudspeaker: "Trailing the field by 15 lengths is Robdale." Dave is frowning with anxiety and starting to sweat. Robdale slowly but steadily catches up to the back of the pack and battles his way toward the middle of the pack. As the horses thunder down the home stretch, the announcer's voice rises in excitement. "And coming up the middle of the track is Robdale!" Dave's cheeks are flushed. His eyes are dilated. He is completely absorbed in the moment. Astoundingly, Robdale wins by a nose. Going into the race, the odds on the horse winning had been 10 to 1. But Dave loves Robdale and he loves long shots. He had bet $3,000 on Robdale and the nail-biting finish delivers a tidy $30,000 in winnings. What a rush of adrenaline for Dave.

Dave intends to enter Robdale in the Kentucky Derby, even though he'll face serious competition from rivals and is an even greater long shot. But in another prep race shortly before Derby Day, the horse next to Robdale kicks him coming out of the gate, chipping his ankle bone. In the aftermath of the incident, Robdale's horse stall is in chaos. The trainer and his assistants, the vet, stable hands, and Dave, Louise, Robin and I all crowd around the horse discussing his future. Dave insists that the horse get the best care possible. The veterinarian operates on Robdale, but his racing days are over. Dave eventually sells him for very little money, and Robdale spends his remaining years at pasture. Now Dave must find another sure bet.

CHAPTER 2: A LONG GAME

As a child, I assume everybody's father is just like my dad. Owning and betting on sleek horses, visiting posh Vegas casinos where everyone knows his name, playing poker with famous entertainers – all this is a normal part of Dave's life and so it's something I take for granted. It comes as a revelation to me that most other kids' fathers are predictable, sometimes downright boring. Sure, sometimes my dad is tense, self-centered and demanding; he can have a short fuse. But to me, compared to Louise, he's the adventurous and exciting parent.

I'm seven years old when we take off on a particularly memorable Dave Zarin adventure. A major snow storm, perhaps the biggest one in years, is blowing into town. Snow or no snow, my father decides he *has* to pick up some documents at his office in Hoboken. It can't wait, he insists. Louise can't talk him out of the expedition. Our family socializes regularly with the Epsteins across the street, so Dave asks Mr. Epstein if he can borrow their station wagon, because it has better tires. Dave also asks me to go along, as well as my buddy, the Epsteins' son Jon. Dave figures that if he gets stuck in the snow, we two will help shovel. Jon and I wear pajamas under our snow suits, so if we fall asleep on the way home, our parents can easily put us to bed.

We set out in the blizzard for Dave's office, about 15 miles away. It takes us hours to cross the Pulaski Skyway, even though the elevated causeway connecting Newark and Jersey City is only about 3 1/2 miles long. The car gets stuck in the snow many times. As nighttime falls, Jon and I are freezing and hungry; we haven't eaten anything all day. Of course, we never make it to the office. Dave ends up driving to Newark Airport for shelter and takes us to the Newarker, the terminal's fancy restaurant. Jon and I, still in our snow suits, take seats at a table bedecked with crisp white napkins and gleaming silverware. Dave goes to the pay phone to call Louise and the Epsteins, who are frenzied with worry by this time. Oblivious to the uproar back home, Jon and I can't wait to tell our friends about our snow storm adventure when we go back to school.

The three Epstein children are close in age to Robin and me. Mr. Epstein owns a small textile mill; his wife Lillian is a vivacious, platinum blonde with a penchant for bright, form-fitting outfits and flashy jewelry. She uses a cigarette holder when she smokes, like a Hollywood femme fatale. She is the polar opposite of my mother, both in personality and appearance. In contrast to Lillian's flamboyance, my mother is demure, and prefers a stylish yet classic look. Her well-put-together outfits – elegant, understated jewelry and carefully coordinated shoes and handbags – only look expensive; she relishes bargain-hunting at Daffy's, a popular discount clothing store similar to TJ Maxx. Though she's proud of her savvy shopping, she cuts the tags off her new purchases so Dave won't see how *little* she has paid. She fears he'll view her bargain shopping as a sign that she lacks confidence in his business prowess.

As Dave's business blossoms, he hires Lillian as his office manager. They work closely together for many years and she becomes Dave's "office wife." They go to Manhattan together for dinner and to meet mutual friends. Lillian, not Louise, is with Dave in New York the first time Dave meets Rich's girlfriend, Susan, the young woman he eventually marries. Lillian and Dave often leave the office in late afternoon for the horse races at Yonkers or Roosevelt, and Lillian even accompanies Dave on one of his Las Vegas trips.

As Dave's gambling obsession grows, Lillian becomes his accomplice. Once, Dave gives her $10,000 to place a bet on a particular horse in the fifth race at Monmouth Racetrack. He tells her to spread the bets across several teller windows to be sure the wagers don't lower the odds. The horse loses. Dave, Lillian later recalls, "loved the excitement and intensity of gambling. He is completely drawn to it, just completely." She adds, somberly, "I think he lived for gambling."

My mother dislikes Lillian. In fact, whenever Lillian's name comes up, Louise's face fleetingly twists into an uncharacteristic sneer. I first assume that tension stems from a simple clash of personalities: Lillian's showy, over-the-top style versus Louise's understated demeanor. I eventually realize there's another reason for my mother's dislike. One evening in my teens, Dave has been out late; we're all waiting for him to get home. From my spot in the dining room where I'm doing homework, I see my mother keeping an eye on the street through the living room window. The glare of headlights down the block catches her eye and she leans forward to watch his blue Buick with its tail fins rolling down the street. A second sedan follows so closely that its front grill reflects the red glare of Dave's tail lights. Dave turns right into our driveway; the other car turns left into the Epstein driveway. I can see my mother wince and recoil when she glimpses Lillian's blond beehive emerge from the driver's side of the Epstein car. Louise hunches her shoulders, turns away from the window and silently walks upstairs.

Occasionally Louise delivers a veiled jab at Lillian in retaliation. On one occasion, Louise and Dave plan to meet Lillian and her husband Eddie at their favorite dinner spot; but Louise and Dave are running late. When they finally arrive at the table, Louise slides into the banquette next to Lillian and whispers an "apology" in her ear: "Sorry for being late, honey. I had the hardest time taking out my diaphragm." She winks playfully at Lillian.

It will take Louise a few more years to begin to understand that the "other woman" isn't a romantic rival. Instead, it's Dave's nearly lifelong love affair with gambling.

Even after the Epsteins move to Short Hills, I remain close friends with Jon. In the summer of 1968, after my first year in college and Jon's second, we decide to travel together to Israel and Europe. We have a limited budget and spend the first four weeks working on a Kibbutz in Israel in exchange for room and board. Each day, we head out to the orchard, sit on ladders across from each other, and discuss our dreams and future plans as we pick pears.

Jon has set his sights on becoming a lawyer. We both know that my father is keen for me to join him in his development business. But as I pull the ripening fruit from the trees, I confide to Jon that I have other dreams. Our trip abroad has opened doors to other cultures and I want a career that enables me to travel the world far beyond New Jersey.

Yet, I *am* still my father's son – at least to some extent. As Jon and I tour Europe, we decide that the casino at

Monte Carlo is on our must-visit list. At a basement bar in what was then West Berlin, we meet a chain-smoking German with nicotine-stained fingers who shares his "can't lose" system of betting at the roulette table. We're immediately intrigued. To win at roulette, we have to correctly bet on which of the 1-36 numbers (colored red or black) the spinning ball would land. Or, we can bet on the color red or black. At that time, Monte Carlo's famed roulette wheel has a pocket marked 0; whenever the ball lands there, everyone loses. (Today, roulette tables have the numbers 0 and 00, both of which belong to the house, tilting the odds even more in favor of the casino.) Betting on either red or black gives the gambler nearly a 50-50 chance of winning. The German guy leans across the table; in a low, conspiratorial tone, he explains the secret to roulette success. Set a base bet, such as a dollar. "Every time you win, take the winning dollar and leave the dollar bet on the table," he explains. "If you lose, double your bet until you win." In this way we'll get our money back, plus $1. If we bet $1, then $2, then $4, for a total of $7, we end up with $8 if we win. Jon and I look at each other; it sounds too simple to be true. We're newbies and don't grasp the real risk with this strategy. If we lose multiple times in a row, and keep doubling our bet, either we end up hitting the betting limit at the table, unable to increase our stake any further, or we run out of money. Needless to say, we can't wait to try this "sure thing" at the roulette tables in Monte Carlo.

The Belle Epoque-era casino is ultra-posh, and backpackers like us stick out amid the elegant patrons. We don't care. We only have about $100 between us, and we need all of it for the final week of our trip. We use $1 as our base bet. The first night is a great success. We win more than $100 and we're ecstatic. We're just as triumphant on the second night. Then, on the third night, our luck changes. After about an hour of play, we lose eight times in a row betting that the ball will end up on a red number. We empty our pockets, and put everything we have, except for $10, on red for a final time. I walk away from the table, unable to watch. Glancing anxiously at Jon a moment later, I see him give me an exultant thumbs up. We beat the odds and now have a few hundred dollars – a fortune! I may be my father's son, but I also know when to quit. We leave the casino immediately.

***

In 1972, the real estate development business slows down dramatically. And yet, Dave continues to gamble heavily at the track and visit Vegas regularly. On one of his particularly bad losing streaks, Dave faces a dire cash crunch. He struggles to pay his employees' salaries and is confronting bankruptcy. He'll have to sell all his assets to raise money. The condominium in Florida goes; so do all the horses. My parents sell their house and move into a two-bedroom apartment in Elizabeth. Dave sells his ownership shares in the nursing homes he built or that are under construction.

One of those projects, the Newark Health and Extended Care Facility, has incurred significant cost overruns during construction. The investors can't put up any more money and neither can Dave. He desperately needs to sell the project. Through a broker, Dave meets a potential buyer, Sol Henkind, a short, balding guy from New York. To Dave's relief, he and Sol agree on a price to acquire the nursing home. But when they meet to finalize the deal, Sol demands that Dave slash the price. He senses Dave's desperation, and uses it to snap up an asset at a deep discount. It feels like a stick up, but Dave has no choice and he folds.

Dave's struggle to resolve his business worries spills over into his personal life. Soon after his fire sale of assets, Dave finds himself unable to repay an investment from a couple who were close friends with him and Louise. He had convinced them to invest in a project and promised to return the money if the project didn't pan out. It doesn't, but Dave can't immediately repay them. The woman then asks Dave to give her Louise's treasured diamond engagement ring as collateral until Dave can pay them back fully.

Louise is shocked and hurt when Dave asks her for the ring. "Some friend!" she cries bitterly. Dave's ashamed but he knows that he has to make good on the debt. It takes him two years to reimburse the couple. Once he repays them, the woman promptly returns the ring to Louise. Their friendship, however, is over. This incident, coming on the heels of so many other disappointments, leaves Louise with an enduring sadness and resentment toward Dave. I also notice that Louise has stopped wearing her cherished ring.

At about the same time, an incident involving Lillian, who is by now divorced, inflicts lasting damage to Dave's relationship with the Epsteins. One afternoon, Rob, Jon's youngest sibling, comes home unannounced from summer camp where he had been working as a junior counselor. He notices a strange car in the driveway, and assumes his mother is having coffee with a friend from her bridge club. He enters the house to find both the living room and dining room deserted.

"Mom, I'm home," he calls out. Climbing the stairs to his bedroom, he hears a flurry of shuffling noises and urgent whispering in his mother's bedroom. The door is closed, so he knocks.

There's a long pause before Lillian answers.

"Oh honey, what a great surprise, I'll be right out,"

A few minutes later, she emerges and closes the door behind her. The deep blush on Lillian's face matches the bright red poppies printed on her silk bathrobe. From inside the bedroom, Rob hears the jingling of pocket change and keys and the rustling sounds of someone hastily dressing. He's just beginning to realize what's going on when Dave flings open the bedroom door, fully dressed.

Dave murmurs a quick good bye and hurries down the stairs and out of the house.

Rob goes into his bedroom and shuts the door.

Lillian and Rob never discuss the incident; soon afterwards, Lillian stops working for Dave and their relationship ends.

CHAPTER 3: A BETTING STRATEGY

In 1974, as Dave is rebuilding his business, Congress authorizes a major housing program, the Housing and Community Development Act. Dave quickly recognizes that this can reinvigorate his business, offering new sources of capital and growth. The new act creates what becomes known as the "Section 8" program, giving low-income senior citizens and low-income tenants a helping hand by capping their share of rent to 30 percent of their income. The federal government will cover the balance. For my father, this is a win-win scenario. Being able to build Section 8 housing offers him great business opportunities. But it's just as important to him that these new multifamily projects can transform the lives of millions of Americans.

Dave is still recovering from having to unload his assets at fire sale prices only a couple of years earlier. In order to build a Section 8 project, he needs to raise new seed capital. In spite of his previous dealings with Sol Henkind, Dave turns to him to provide the money for his first venture into this new kind of housing in Allentown, Pennsylvania. Sol agrees to invest enough money for Dave to operate an office, acquire the land, prepare architectural designs and engineering plans, obtain regulatory approvals and put up the letters of credit to get below-market rate financing from tax exempt bonds issued by the Pennsylvania Housing Finance Agency. That project, a

160-unit senior citizen high-rise apartment, is completed in 1977. It's the first of its kind in the United States.

Dave now has proved that building affordable multifamily and senior citizen housing is a viable business. The model involves obtaining both public and private financing at below-market interest rates, a model that appeals to a tax syndicator such as the National Housing Partnership. NHP, or similar entities, buy most of the shares in the project and sell interests to individual investors as pass-through tax deductions. Dave and his partners receive development fees paid by NHP and other investors in installments over several years, according to a schedule. It turns into a win-win-*win* scenario.

Dave quickly begins planning other Section 8 housing projects throughout Pennsylvania and embarks on one in Florida. Opening a small office in Harrisburg, Pennsylvania, he assembles a very skilled project development team. But Dave remains a very hands on CEO. He understands every detail of each project. He supervises the purchase of the land and the drafting of engineering specifications and architectural designs. He also navigates the regulatory issues and approvals and pieces together complex financings. Dave thinks ten steps ahead, anticipating pitfalls long before anyone else spots them. Though he delegates a lot of responsibility to his team, he always knows what they are doing. He's a demanding boss. Anyone working for him – employees, consultants or lawyers – knows to be ready for a call from Dave asking about a given project at any hour of the day or night, seven days a week.

Dave's attention to detail is almost obsessive. Any time a new tenant moves into one of the residential projects that he owns, Dave insists that apartment unit not only be cleaned but upgraded with fresh paint and new carpeting. Sometimes he inspects the work himself to make sure it meets his standards. If he spots a blemish or bump on newly painted walls, he scratches at it and growls at the maintenance crew; they touch it up on the spot. This kind of single-mindedness enables Dave to build and sell more than 1,500 Section 8 senior and multifamily housing units between 1977 and 1980, valued at $40 million, or $182 million in 2024 dollars.

Dave frequently tells me that he doesn't care about money; it's only one way to measure success or failure. But by this standard, he's finally on the road to success. Still, Dave is a difficult business partner to work with. His approach to risk-taking in business in many ways mirrors his risk-taking in gambling. Dave is relentless. In negotiations with an investor or partner, or even with a government agency, he's willing to put the entire project at risk to get the other party to capitulate on an issue he considers critical to the success of the project.

Dave now decides to set up a separate company to manage all the housing projects he's building. In 1977 he asks my brother Rich to run the management company as a partner. By now, Rich is 33 years old, with two small children. He has a Master's degree in health administration from Columbia and is a deputy commissioner in the Pennsylvania Department of Health. They form an odd partnership: Rich, a risk-averse administrator, must try to rein in Dave, the daring risk taker. In retrospect, Rich was ill-suited for the rough and tumble real estate development world that enthralled Dave. Their prior arguments, particularly over Dave's treatment of Louise, add another layer of complexity to the new business relationship.

Just as Dave and Rich form the new property management company that Rich will run, new opportunities and challenges, both personal and professional, loom for Dave. The focus of all the excite-ment? The fact that New Jersey legislators are debating sweeping changes to the state's gambling laws.

As far back as the 1920s, Atlantic City, with its long sand-swept boardwalk and bustling shops, rolling ocean and wide beaches, had been a favorite vacation spot for many families in the New York and mid-Atlantic region. Beginning in the late 1950s and early 1960s, the U.S. interstate highway network makes longer car trips smoother and faster and later the airline industry expands. This growth enables families to begin vacationing further afield. Instead of heading for Atlantic City, they travel to New England or head south to Florida and the Caribbean. Even Dave and Louise prefer to vacation in Florida.

As a result, by the 1970s Atlantic City's tourism industry is in freefall. Decaying attractions, boarded-up storefronts, ramshackle houses and weed-strewn vacant lots are a blight on what was once a quaint, lively and appealing beachfront community. The municipal govern-ment, plagued by corruption, proves itself incapable of slowing the city's decline. By 1974, Atlantic City is a shadow of its former self; the boardwalk is a ghost town. Many of the city's venerable hotels are tired-looking, dilapidated or closed. The further visitors venture beyond the boardwalk, the more depressing the city looks: an unappealing spectacle of abandoned houses, seedy pawn shops and adult 'entertainment' stores. Only a few restaurants remain. As younger people leave the city for better jobs and a better quality of life, the exodus further hollows out Atlantic City.

Those who remain do so because they have no alternative: They are predominantly poor, elderly, or underemployed people of color. The city is in an economic death spiral.

In a bold effort to revive and revitalize the city, local business leaders and politicians discuss bringing casino gambling to Atlantic City. One of the most respected politicians leading the effort is 26-year-old Steve Perskie, elected in 1971 to the New Jersey State Assembly to represent Atlantic City and surrounding areas. Perskie, a thin man of medium height, with curly brown hair, mustache and 70s-era aviator-style glasses, has a politician's winning smile and infectious optimism. Perskie supported Brendan Byrne for governor in 1973 and developed a close working relationship with the new governor's staff after Byrne's victory. He wins Byrne's tacit support for casino gambling in the state.

At this time, New Jersey's constitution prohibits all forms of gaming. Bringing a casino to Atlantic City will require state legislators to amend the constitution, but even before they can tackle that task, they must win voter approval in a referendum. In 1974, Perskie works with State Senator Joe McGahn to craft legislation permitting a limited number of state-owned – rather than privately owned - casinos to operate in Atlantic City. To garner enough votes, they decide to word the bill to permit casino gambling anywhere in the state. The state's voters soundly reject the measure in a 1974 election referendum. But Perskie, like Dave, isn't the kind of guy to take "no" for an answer.

When Perskie wins reelection to the Assembly for a third term in 1975, he promptly resumes discussions about another casino gambling referendum. Perskie makes his case with the governor and his staff, local politicians, and hotel and business leaders, including members of Atlantic City's substantial Black community. This time, he and McGahn propose a less ambitious plan, one that limits casino gambling to Atlantic City. They also open the doors to the private sector becoming involved. As a sweetener, they recommend that some of the gaming industry proceeds be dedicated to housing and services for senior citizens and the disabled.

Atlantic City's political, business, and civic leaders establish a Committee to Rebuild Atlantic City (with the unfortunate acronym of "CRAC") to coordinate the campaign. CRAC drives the statewide messaging and advertising for the referendum in the run-up to the 1976 election.

Resorts International, which owns and operates a casino in the Bahamas, gets involved as well. The company has been looking for ways to expand its reach to the U.S. and believes that the revised proposition has a decent chance of being approved in a new referendum. Resorts makes a huge bet by snapping up property along the boardwalk in Atlantic City months before the referendum takes place, gambling that it will be able to use the land to establish a casino hotel. In August 1976, Resorts purchases the Chalfonte-Haddon Hall Hotel, a renowned but now decrepit 1920's-era 1,000-room boardwalk hotel, for $2.5 million. The gaming company immediately begins to design a complete renovation. It also donates $250,000 to CRAC to support the referendum. Resorts' foresight gives the company a year-long head start over its rivals as Atlantic City moves closer to becoming the country's next gambling center. Established casino operators in Las Vegas watch the New

Jersey debate warily. Until now, Nevada has been the only U.S. state permitting casinos to operate, and Vegas casino owners worry that Atlantic City will siphon off some of their customers.

In 1976, Perskie drafts the "Casino Control Act of 1976". If voters approve gaming in the referendum, state lawmakers will introduce the bill immediately. At the same time, he and others tour New Jersey, making the case for casinos to individual voters and groups. Their message is clear: A thriving gaming industry will restore the luster to the onetime gem of the Jersey shore. Their efforts pay off. On November 2, 1976, the citizens of New Jersey vote to legalize gambling in Atlantic City, and legislators promptly approve Perskie's already-prepared legislation.

Expectations soar for the renewal and revitalization of the city. Atlantic City remains ideally located for day-trippers up and down the Eastern Seaboard. At least 37.5 million people live within a four-hour drive of the beachfront community. While a trip to Vegas involves a long and expensive flight from the East Coast, it takes only 60 minutes to reach Atlantic City from Philadelphia by car, and a mere two hours from New York. What's more, the city's marina attracts affluent boaters.

The new legislation triggers an immediate land rush in Atlantic City and makes real estate speculation feel like just another casino game. Overnight, anyone owning land on or near the boardwalk becomes a millionaire, at least on paper. Property values increase tenfold or more between 1976 and 1980, as speculators option land and resell those options several times over at ever-higher prices. In land option contracts, a landowner agrees to sell property at a stipulated price to a potential buyer (developer) within a specified length of time. If the buyer doesn't purchase the property within that time frame, the seller then can turn around and find a new buyer, for either the land or the option.

By 1983, the price of land per square foot is higher in certain areas of Atlantic City than in Manhattan. This makes those who own land in the run-down city seem like brilliant investors, as rising prices wipe out their previous losses and turn them into real estate moguls. But this rampant speculation also sharply reduces the housing supply. Landlords evict long-time tenants from older homes, then sell the buildings for the value of the land to developers who proceed to tear them down. Suspicious fires break out in a number of neighborhoods, destroying the increasingly meager supply of housing. Dave clearly recognizes that the arrival of gambling is triggering the mass displacement of the very workforce the new casinos will rely on to function and to thrive.

"There'll be thousands of new hires in the casinos," Dave tells Rich. "Custodians, servers, croupiers, dealers and managers – they all need to live *somewhere* that's affordable and comfortable." If it's done right, he adds, the city's redevelopment could serve as a national model for revitalization. And Dave is convinced he can lead the way. He begins to mobilize his team.

The city is moving at warp speed and Dave leaps on board the train.

CHAPTER 4: THE OPENING BET

In March 1978, Dave brings his team to Atlantic City and begins to hold staff meetings in his new "office." It's a small suite at Resorts, which has just opened its non-casino hotel section. Dave has a history with Resorts; he spent time gambling at its Bahamas casino and in 1975 lost $20,000 at the tables there. Now, having paid off the remainder of that debt, he persuades the fledgling Atlantic City casino to provide him with a complimentary hotel suite as he gets his new business up and running. Resorts no doubt considers the "comped" room to be a good investment. When the casino opens for business, both Resorts and Dave expect he'll be a regular player at its craps tables. In the interim, Dave sets his sights on becoming a big player in Atlantic City's development gold rush.

In one of their earliest staff meetings in Dave's suite, Rich and Dave unfurl a map of Atlantic City on a round conference table. Joining them and bending over the table to study it closely, are Dave's project manager Ken Smith, his long-time civil engineer, Lou Adler, and Bill Rafferty, one of the most knowledgeable and well-regarded real estate brokers in the city. Rafferty explains the current status of city zoning and land acquisition, using the tip of his pencil to point to different locations on the map as he does so. Thanks to his excellent contacts at city hall, he has a good idea of what the city's zoning master plan will look like. Situated on a barrier island, the city is only 48 blocks long and extends only 10 blocks at its widest. Rafferty taps the pencil eraser on the map.

"The resort development district, where the casinos must be built, will be only along the boardwalk and in the Marina, an area northwest of the boardwalk on the Absecon Inlet," he says. These sections are the most appealing to tourists. Other neighborhoods, such as Ducktown and Chelsea, are principally white, middle-class enclaves, Rafferty explains.

"And then there's the dying Atlantic City business district along Atlantic Avenue which parallels the boardwalk." Rafferty traces his pencil the length of the thoroughfare. "The plan calls for it to remain commercial."

Dave asks which areas would be suitable for his affordable housing projects. Rafferty moves his pencil to indicate Northside, a predominantly Black and working-class neighborhood, then identifies other parts of town with similar demographics.

"These are likely to be zoned for multifamily residential develop-ment," he says. "These are blighted areas, with boarded-up or burned-out vacant properties."

But that doesn't mean this land will be easy to acquire, Rafferty warns. Speculators have driven up the price, he says, shaking his head. Option prices are soaring, even in these poorer communities.

"The problem will be to accumulate enough adjacent parcels, at an affordable price, to build high-rise and low-rise multifamily housing. Each street is broken up into many individual lots," he says, frowning.

"You may need to buy eight or nine individual adjacent lots if you're going to assemble enough land to build on. This isn't going to be cheap."

There is one site that might work well in the short term, Rafferty adds, pointing to land bordering on Mediterranean Avenue and Tennessee Avenue in the Northside neighborhood.

"You could probably buy enough land there to begin building rapidly. However…" Rafferty pauses. "However, there's a guy who lives in the town of Ventnor and owns several gas stations. He began buying up lots on this block right after the referendum passed," Rafferty sighs. "I hear he now owns the options to buy all the lots on the entire block. He's going to ask for a lot of money for this."

Getting hold of the land is just the first hurdle. Dave knows that to build any multifamily housing, he will need permits and approval by the planning board. Getting these is a very political process, further complicated by land speculators who, like the investor from Ventnor, don't even live in Atlantic City. Their sole goal is making money; unlike Dave, they don't care about improving the quality of life in Atlantic City. Still, without the land, Dave can't get started. He studies the map carefully.

"Bill, I need you to buy this block immediately, whatever it costs." He jabs his finger at the spot on the map. "This could be our first project in Atlantic City." Dave raises his chin and straightens his back. "Then, I need you to come up with a strategy to buy up individual lots." Eventually, he argues, the team can cobble them together into a plot large enough for a new multi-family housing project. As the men discuss next steps, they're swept up by the same sense of excitement and optimism that Dave feels at the craps table.

As Dave's Atlantic City team gets to work, he still pursues projects and deals elsewhere. On April 15, 1978, Dave is at the Jockey Club in Miami to meet an attorney to discuss a possible housing project in Miami. The Jockey Club is one of the swankiest social clubs in the city, with a well-known bar, restaurant and hotel, and the sophisticated, high-quality amenities and services catering to movie stars and the international jet set.

Early that evening, after his meeting wraps up, Dave sits at the elegant wood-paneled bar sipping his second martini. Mulling his myriad real estate projects, he barely registers the room's sumptuous décor or its dramatic views of Biscayne Bay. He's deep in thought when suddenly a woman he doesn't know plunks a plate of shrimp down in front of him.

"You look like you need something to eat," she says with a hint of a smile. "That must be your second or third martini." Startled, Dave looks up at a tall woman regarding him intently.

"This is my second, actually. But who's counting?" Dave says, looking down at his drink. The woman climbs onto the barstool next to him and extends a manicured hand sparkling with two large diamond rings. "I'm Martha Nemtin."

Dave shakes her hand and looks at her appraisingly, judging her to be in her mid-fifties. At first glance, he doesn't find the woman particularly attractive. She's what polite company might call "big boned." Her small brown eyes are set closely together above a long nose, though her full lips and the flattering cut of her dark curly hair soften the angles of her square face. His eyes quickly survey her expensive jewelry and Ferragamo shoes and handbag, all of which denote both wealth and good taste.

Martha immediately launches into a monologue, telling Dave about herself.

"I have a successful real estate practice in Montreal, and run my business out of my apartment," she says, with a smile and more than a hint of pride in her voice. "It's very successful. I support myself."

That gets Dave's attention; he wants to hear more.

"I have a teenage son who has a learning disability. He lives with me. He's at home." Martha pauses to order a glass of wine. "I'm meeting my sister here for dinner. She lives in Miami with her family," she adds. "I'm divorced."

She stops abruptly. "So, tell me about these business problems keeping you so preoccupied that you've forgotten to eat."

Dave is intrigued by the wealthy, successful business-woman who seems genuinely interested in his work and achievements. He's always wanted to have someone in his life with whom he can discuss the intricacies and pressures of putting together complicated housing projects. His wife? Certainly not. What matters to Louise is their family, not his business.

Rich? His son may be a partner in some ways, but their business discussions are more general in scope, or else focus on the minutiae of day-to-day property management in Pennsylvania. Dave often takes business risks or extends himself financially in ways that make Rich uncomfortable, if not downright anxious.

Dave begins to warm to Martha; here is someone smart, ambitious, successful – and interested. The floodgates open. For the next hour, Dave talks about his housing projects in Pennsylvania and his vision for Atlantic City.

"It's going to bring incredible benefits to ordinary people who can't find affordable homes anymore." Dave shifts in his seat. "I just need to figure out how to navigate the politics." He signals for another round of drinks.

When Martha's sister arrives an hour later, Dave invites them both to dinner at Joe's Stone Crab, a trendy restaurant he patronizes whenever he's in Miami. In contrast to dinners with Louise, who listens in silence as Dave talks about his projects, Martha asks pointed, thoughtful questions and offers shrewd observations peppered with witty anecdotes about her own business experiences.

The two engage in an animated back and forth that Dave finds seductive. This woman clearly has a firm grasp of business issues, and good judgment, Dave thinks to himself. When she speaks, he catches himself watching her lips. She discusses topics that matter to him with a confidence and wit that he finds sexy. Martha meanwhile has done everything but hold up a billboard to signal her interest in Dave. After dinner, Martha's sister goes home alone. Martha accompanies Dave to his room at the Jockey Club and spends the night.

The next morning over a breakfast of eggs, toast and coffee, Martha says that she knows someone in Montreal who might own property in Atlantic City. Perhaps this would be helpful for Dave? She calls her friend and sets up a meeting in Atlantic City for a few weeks later. Still enjoying the afterglow of the previous evening, Dave wants to pursue a relationship with Martha and asks her to join him in New York for the weekend. Together they spend a long weekend at the Plaza Hotel and take in dinner at Tavern on the Green, fabled places that Martha only knows about from magazines and the movies.

During this romantic getaway, the couple still discuss business. Martha confides that business in Montreal is very slow and she's restless.

"I need to find something new that I can sink my teeth into," she says, then pauses. "Maybe I can help you acquire land in Atlantic City." Although her son lives with her, she tells Dave she could spend as much as three days a week in Atlantic City.

Dave jumps at the chance to work with her. They decide that her first visit will be to participate in the meeting with the Canadian businessman. She'll then stay on to help Dave buy other property.

It turns out her friend's property won't work for multifamily housing, but by now it doesn't really matter. Martha is becoming Dave's constant companion in Atlantic City. He arranges for Resorts to offer her a comped room adjoining his own. Like Lillian before her, Martha becomes Dave's new "office wife" – with benefits.

***

Almost no one has a kind word to say about Atlantic City's local government. The city's improved fortunes only deepen public mistrust among its 40,000 residents. Dave quickly realizes that Mayor Joseph Lazarow, a short, stocky man with brown hair, glasses and a double chin, simply isn't up to the challenge of such rapid and large-scale development. Nor are most of the city commissioners. With one exception: Housing Commissioner Pierre Hollingsworth, a tall, soft-spoken, Black man with a thin mustache, and a statesman-like manner. He also heads up the local chapter of the NAACP and has been the city's deputy fire chief. Crucially, he's a passionate advocate of affordable housing and highly regarded by the Black community, which makes up about 40 percent of the city's population.

In early May, Dave drops by City Hall to meet Pierre, whose large desk is cluttered with stacks of paper and files. Dave is tall, but Hollingsworth looms over him as they shake hands.

"I've heard a lot of good things about you," Dave says. "I hope we can work together to build affordable housing."

Pierre raises his eyebrows in surprise. He smiles as he motions to Dave to take a seat.

"Well, you're the first developer to tell me *that* since I've been in this office." Pierre says. He takes a chair near Dave. "If you really mean it, I'd be eager to work with you. But start off by telling me what you have in mind."

Dave wastes no time in describing his vision for housing. Combining federal Section 8 subsidies and casino gambling tax revenues present a unique opportunity for affordable housing financing and development, he tells Pierre.

"We can make a huge and immediate difference in the lives of the people of Atlantic City," Dave says. He describes his Allentown project, and the more than 1,000 affordable housing units for seniors and families that he's already built. More are in the pipeline. This isn't just his business, Dave tells Pierre. He's determined to transform Atlantic City.

"Pierre, I need persistent, vocal community backing, especially from the Black community, for our plans to work," Dave explains. He knows that Pierre wields a lot of influence in the city and his advocacy is crucial.

"I need help to identify and acquire land at a reasonable price, to get zoning and planning board approvals and permits. I'll need local, state and federal government support," he adds "Can I count on your help?"

Pierre is well aware of Atlantic City's dire need of affordable housing and he hears what he believes to be genuine commitment and conviction in Dave's voice. Reaching a sudden decision, he stands up.

"Let's go for a ride," he says. "I'll show you neighborhoods you should look at closely."

They get into Pierre's Oldsmobile and set out along the Atlantic Avenue business district.

"I bet there's a lot about Atlantic City history that you haven't heard before," Pierre tells Dave, as he drives. "This city has been segregated during most of its early history. Black people worked menial jobs at all of the hotels, but there was only a single beach where they were welcome to relax, swim and picnic. It came to be known as 'Chicken Bone Beach'."

Pierre grimaces at the name. Even after segregation ended, discriminatory practices like red-lining confined the Black community to the 80 square blocks that make up the Northside neighborhood.

"That's the area we're driving through now." Pierre points toward the street as they turn onto Baltic Avenue. "This neighborhood used to be one of the premier African American communities in the Northeast. A thriving area, full of businesses, doctors' offices. School teachers lived here in nice townhouses."

Northside also had been an entertainment mecca for Black Americans who flocked to Atlantic City in droves.

"Black-owned hotels like this used to flourish," Pierre says as he pulls up alongside an aging six-story brick building displaying a faded sign that reads "Liberty Hotel." It's clearly seen better days. The Liberty opened in the 1930s and had been a leading hotel catering to well-to-do Black vacationers, artists, musicians and writers. Pierre's expression grows somber; his voice softens. "At one time, this was one of the pearls of Atlantic City."

He leads Dave into the hotel where a thin Black man is leaning over the front desk reading the newspaper. A worn brown couch occupies one corner of the linoleum-tiled lobby.

"James, how many guests do you have today?" Pierre inquires. Turning around, James counts the keys hanging on hooks in front of room numbers.

"Eleven guests," he responds. "Five are monthly; the rest are weekly."

Pierre turns to Dave. "I want you to think about turning this building into affordable housing."

Pierre then takes Dave on a quick tour of other historic buildings, now boarded up, that for years served the city's once-thriving Black community. In the car, Pierre watches as Dave scribbles down each address they visit.

"Do you think any of these buildings could be turned into affordable housing?" Pierre asks.

"Yes." Dave says, without hesitation. "I don't see why it can't be done. I'll get my engineer and architect in here to take a look."

Pierre turns in his seat to look Dave straight in the eye.

"If you can convert these buildings into affordable housing," he says slowly, emphasizing each word, "then I'll know you're for real. Then you'll have my full support and I'll do everything I can to get the Black community to support you."

"It's a deal," Dave says. They shake hands on what would become a deep, lifelong collaboration and friendship.

In early May, as Dave and Pierre agree to join forces, it's still unclear whether Resorts will be able to open its casino on schedule by Memorial Day. The New Jersey Division of Gaming Enforcement is still conducting its background investigation into all of the officers, principal stockholders and affiliated companies of Resorts. Any sign of financial problems, mismanagement or links to organized crime, and Resorts won't get the license to begin operations. But the process is taking a long time, and is nowhere near complete as Memorial Day approaches.

New Jersey's political leaders, including Governor Byrne, also feel pressure to launch casino operations by the beginning of the summer season. With their last-minute legislative support, the state grants Resorts a temporary operating permit in the nick of time. After investing nearly $30 million in renovating the Chalfonte-Haddon Hall Hotel, the new five-star Resorts casino opens with great fanfare and a lot of media coverage on Friday May 26, even though its permanent casino license is still pending.

The residents of Atlantic City – and people from all over the East Coast – can't wait to get inside the doors. A line begins forming on the sidewalk outside the casino the night before, as VIPs and Resorts executives gather indoors for a lavish celebration. Headlining the entertainment that night are the husband-and-wife singers Steve Lawrence and Edie Gorme. Guests include a who's who of New Jersey state officials and politicians: Governor Byrne, most state legislators, all of the state cabinet officials and most local politicians. Steve Perskie, now a state senator, serves as master of ceremonies. The governor tells the audience that Atlantic City is making history by reclaiming its crown as "the queen of resorts."

The next morning, Byrne, Resorts President Jack Davis, James Crosby, the chairman of Resorts, and many local politicians attend the ribbon-cutting at the casino's entrance. By that time, thousands of people are lined up waiting to get in. Many are wearing their best attire: Men in suit jackets and polished shoes, women in high heels and dresses. The line stretches for four blocks along the boardwalk; as the locals are joined by visitors from New York, Chicago and even California. Ringed by cameras and reporters, the governor cuts the ribbon.

"My father always told me never to bet on anything except Notre Dame and the New York Yankees," he jokes to the crowd. "For those of you who aren't willing to follow my father's advice, the casino is now open!"

The opinion page of The Press, the Atlantic City newspaper, features a headline "A Dream Comes True." In the editorial, the paper gushes that "Atlantic City has recaptured the glamour." In an historic black and white photo, Steve Lawrence is shown leaning over a craps table, tossing the first roll of the dice. Standing beside him is Steve Perskie.

The Resorts Casino's renovation of the old Boardwalk hotel is pitch-perfect. It captures the opulence and atmosphere of the high-end casinos in Las Vegas, while at the same time honoring the unique history of Atlantic City. Dealers wear crisp white shirts, bright multicolored vests and bow ties. Cocktail waitresses in short, lowcut dresses glide around the tables serving free drinks. Casinos deliberately design their layout in a maze to keep gamblers at the tables and slot machines for longer. The gaming floor has no windows and no clocks. In the subdued lighting, players can easily lose track of time. Food and drinks, even rest rooms, are situated just off the casino floor. Plush, colorfully patterned carpeting muffles the sounds of chiming slot machines, clicking roulette wheels, and cheering gamblers winning jackpots.

The level of excitement at the entrance resembles a Saturday night at New York's Studio 54. Burly security guards in dark suits stand by velvet ropes blocking the entry; and they grant admission to new customers only when other players leave. Within 20 minutes of the casino's opening, the crowd inside swells to more than 5,000 persons. They stand three or four deep around the gaming tables and form lines of five or six to play the slots. An elderly lady sitting at the $1 slots hits the jackpot and shrieks gleefully as silver coins rain into her tray. Excited patrons turn an area just off the main casino floor into a huge disco, dancing to the BeeGees soundtrack of Saturday Night Fever.

Resorts President Jack Davis, a taciturn business type, looks out at the crowds with an uncharacteristically broad smile.

He leans toward Governor Byrne's ear, speaking over the din of voices and slot machines, "We think this will be the busiest casino in the world." Byrne, equally jubilant, replies, "It's a new lease on life for Atlantic City."

They're right – at least for a while. The casino takes in more money from slots that Memorial Day weekend than any other casino has ever earned in gambling history. Between 75,000 to 100,000 people visit the casino each day over that three-day weekend. During June 1978, the casino's average daily winnings exceed $750,000, setting a worldwide record in gambling revenue. In its initial three months of operation, Resorts' winnings total $62.8 million, more than any Las Vegas casino has pulled in over a similar period.

Resorts' overnight success isn't lost on any of its Vegas-based rivals. The day after Resorts opens its doors, Stephen Wynn, chairman of the Golden Nugget Companies, walks along the boardwalk looking for property he can expand (or tear down) to build his own casino hotel. He eyes the Strand Motel and Restaurant on Boston Avenue on the boardwalk, a run-down two-story motel with a pool in the middle. He walks into the motel and asks to speak to the owner, who happens to be in the restaurant. Only 25 minutes later, Wynn cuts a deal to purchase the property for $8.5 million in an all-cash transaction. He will tear down the motel and fast-track the development of the Golden Nugget casino with plans to open in 1980.

Amid all the hoopla about Atlantic City's new identity as a casino mecca, an article deep inside the Press, the local newspaper, offers readers a more sober view of the gaming industry. It reports that the National Council on Compulsive Gambling warns that, as the world's first commuter casino, Atlantic City risks becoming a haven for compulsive players. It also notes that Gamblers Anonymous plans to open an office in Atlantic City and that the American Medical Association has designated compulsive gambling as a serious illness, putting it in the same category as drug and alcohol addiction.

It's unlikely that Governor Byrne, Perskie or many of the politicians who battled to pass the casino referendum are worried about these risks, if they're even aware of them. Their goal is to ignite an economic recovery in Atlantic City – and they feel their job is done. Now they'll leave it to market forces to spread the bounty of casino revenues throughout Atlantic City.

That's a misguided assumption, however. Casino operators design their venues specifically to keep patrons on the casino floor or at least within the hotel. They aim to supply all of a customer's needs for food and entertainment on the premises, hiring top-flight chefs and bringing in stars to perform. Casinos want to be self-contained full service resorts, to maximize profit. It turns out that there is little, if any, trickle-down economic effect capable of revitalizing Atlantic City, at least in the absence of active government involvement in its further development. Dave understands this; others don't: Spreading the benefits of casino investment to the entire community requires a strategy and flawless tactical planning. Dave makes it his mission to lead the charge on the housing front.

CHAPTER 5: THE HOUSE EDGE

Dave travels back to Atlantic City on June 11, 1978. As he checks in, he glances at his watch. He's running late and has back-to-back meetings scheduled that day. But instead of heading for the elevators, he rushes off to the casino floor. This is his first time in the casino since it opened on Memorial Day weekend. It's still morning, but the air in the casino is already blue with cigarette smoke. Dave spots a heavy-set man in his 40s approaching him.

"Hi Irv!" Dave calls out. Irv Rogers, the vice president for casino development, knows Dave from his gambling days at Resorts' flagship casino in the Bahamas and authorized "comping" Dave's small suite at the hotel and other perks. Looking again at his watch, Dave wastes little time. "Irv, I'm planning to play later, but I'd like to arrange a $10,000 credit line now so it's all set up when I get back."

Irv hears the urgency in Dave's voice and knows better than to start small talk when a high roller is jonesing to play.

"Sure, come with me," he says. Weaving rapidly through the crowds, he leads Dave over to the cashier's cage, where the casino keeps its money, chips, credit applications and transaction records. He introduces Dave to Gary Thompson, the cage manager responsible for taking a customer's credit application and running required credit checks. Dave dashes through the application, then sprints off to his next meeting.

While Dave is physically present during the hours that follow, his team notices he's distracted in his meetings. Time seems to drag on; he tries to focus, but feels the pull of the craps table and the cheers that erupt when players win.

Meanwhile, Gary is doing his due diligence into Dave's credit history and opens the Dave Zarin credit file. In it, the casino will meticulously track his gambling activity. The credit check includes a call to Dave's bank for a six-month account history; then to a central clearing house in Las Vegas that collects customer credit reports from every casino in the U.S. According to Resorts in the Bahamas, Dave had owed the casino $20,000 from 1973 until very recently. But Gary isn't worried. He approves Dave's application and walks it over to Irv, who approves Dave's request for a credit limit of $10,000.

Gary prepares Dave's Player Credit Reference Card. This lists his credit limit and ultimately will include a running total of his credit history, the markers he signs, the date and amount of each personal check he writes, any deposits or returned items, as well as bank reports. The card will also note any time another casino checks Dave's credit through the clearing house in Las Vegas. Now that the card is set up, Dave can start gambling.

***

Martha flies into Atlantic City that afternoon and checks into her separate room at Resorts. After a massage and a fresh manicure in the hotel spa, she meets Dave at the hotel's Capriccio restaurant for an early dinner. Martha talks, animatedly and at length, about a pending real estate deal in Montreal as Dave eats in silence. He's anxious to start playing and doesn't linger over the meal or wait for coffee. He hurries to the casino floor, Martha following behind him as he makes a beeline to Irv.

"Are we good to go?" Dave asks.

"Absolutely," Irv said. "I remember you like to play craps. Let's go meet the pit boss."

Martha's eyebrows shoot up in reaction to the casino executive's deference. A satisfied smile spreads across her face as she follows Dave and Irv to meet the pit boss, sitting in a high chair overlooking six craps tables. He's in his late 40s, dressed in a muted brown suit and light blue tie.

"Sam Eller, I'd like you to meet David Zarin," Irv says. "Dave's got a credit limit of $10,000 with us."

Irv's eyes lock with Sam's for a second before he turns to look at Dave.

"Dave and I go back many years, to when he played at our casino in the Bahamas," Irv adds.

Sam nods in understanding, and smiles broadly at Dave.

"Glad to meet you, Mr. Z," he says, as he climbs down from his perch. "Do you mind my calling you that? Mr. Z is easier for me to remember." When Dave introduces Martha, Sam nods again in greeting, and walks them over to the best spot at one of the crap tables.

"How much would you like to start with?" Sam asks.

"Let's start small," Dave says. "Just $500."

Sam turns to a man in a dark suit and tie. "Tony here is your boxman. He'll get you started."

Sam notices the quizzical look on Martha's face. "The boxman dispenses chips in exchange for the players' cash," Sam tells her. "He's like the game's banker."

Martha admires the quality of Tony's tailoring. "He's certainly dressed for the part," she says smiling.

"Tony, please prepare a marker for Mr. Z for $500." Sam turns again to Martha to explain. "A marker is like a check the casino can deposit in the bank for repayment. Though usually, a player just pays off the marker with his winning chips or a personal check."

Tony hands Dave the marker form for him to fill out and sign. Dave's credit reference card will now list his available credit as $9,500.

As Dave surveys the craps table, he nods to the two dealers sporting colorful brocade vests and green bow ties. His pulse quickens as he hears the come-hither clack of chips pushed together. He feasts his eyes on the table's bright new green felt, and fingers the clean leather and mahogany trim.

Martha studies the table's green lining, which displays a confusing array of grid lines and numbers. She waits for Dave to explain the layout to her, but he's already placing his bets. One of the dealers slides $500 worth of $10 and $25 chips to Dave, who stacks them sideways in the grooved rail on the table's edge. Suddenly remembering that Martha is standing beside him, Dave counts out four $25 chips and moves them to her section of the rail. "Here, you'll need to play to stand at the table," he explains.

"But I don't know how to play craps," she says, surprising herself with the tentative tone of her voice. Martha is out of her element, unused to not being in control. And she doesn't like it. She's even more anxious when Dave says, "I'll teach you. It's fun."

The croupier, or stickman, deploys a long, hooked rod to move the dice around the table. He puts five dice on the table and moves them clockwise to the next player, or shooter. Dave places a $25 chip on the Pass line. He turns to Martha and gives her a brief summary of the game. "A bet on the Pass line will win if the shooter, on his initial roll, rolls the number 7 or 11, and will lose if the shooter rolls the numbers 2, 3, or 12. After that, though, I lose whatever I have on the table if a 7 turns up. Just remember that the casino has an edge on the odds."

Martha arches her eyebrows. If the casino weights the odds in its favor, what's the point of gambling? She stops herself from asking. She sees the intense look on Dave's face. He stands commandingly over his chips. After a few rolls, he's ahead.

Then he tells the dealer: "Full press." He turns to Martha. "I doubled up on my bet on the number 6, which pays odds of 7 to 6."

Martha, herself no slouch when it comes to numbers, is impressed by Dave's encyclopedic knowledge of the odds. She signals a waitress and orders a glass of wine. The waitress brings it quickly and slips it deftly onto the small shelf before her. It's a nice Sancerre, on the house, for Mr. Z's friend.

Martha's beginning to understand the game and finds herself fascinated by Dave's bold, aggressive bets. She's way too cautious with her own money to follow suit. She doesn't have the stomach for that kind of risk. But the fact that Dave does, makes him even more desirable in her eyes. Dave's too smart to take risks he can't afford, she tells herself.

"I could really get used to this," Martha thinks to herself as she takes a sip of the Sancerre. The casino certainly wants to keep Dave happy. They like his business, sure, but she can see they also like him. Martha catches the admiring looks directed at Dave by the eight other players watching him. In craps, Dave displays the same panache and energy that he brings to his business.

"And that's why he's so successful, and so rich," Martha tells herself. "And he's with me." She smiles and takes another sip of wine as Dave wins another round.

Three hours later, Dave and Martha are still at the craps table. Dave has enjoyed a string of wins before his luck changes on a dime. Now he's losing steadily. He signs an additional marker for $1,000 and then another for $1,000 more. Then the fourth marker of the evening, for another $500.

Now, Dave's the shooter. His luck turns again and he rolls a series of winning bets. With each hit on a number, he doubles up (or "presses") his wager on that number. Martha orders another glass of wine to calm herself. Although Dave has barely touched his drink, his face is flushed; he bounces lightly on the balls of his feet as his excitement grows.

"Full press," he tells the dealer again. Dave also places one of Martha's $25 chips on number 9. Dave shoots. Everyone around the tables fixes their eyes on the red dice as they bounce and land.

"Seven!" calls the dealer. A chorus of groans erupts, but Dave shows no emotion as the dealer rakes away his pile of chips.

"I think we should go," he says quietly. Martha drains her glass and follows him to the cashier's cage where Dave redeems his chips. A total of $175. After his first day at the craps table, he's in the hole for $3,000, a lot of money in 1978.

As Dave and Martha leave, Sam, the pit boss, fills out the casino's rating form for Mr. Z. Sam notes how long Dave played and the size of his bets. Based on that, the credit manager assigns Dave a rating of 2 on a scale of 1 to 5; 1 is the highest rating. That figure means that Resorts now considers Dave to be a VIP player. Sam fills out another form with estimates of Dave's wins and losses, then adds that data into its Red Book, an informal diary of a player's estimated daily wins and losses. Dave's credit reference card records his markers – totaling $3,000 – which reduces his available credit line to $7,000.

The next evening Dave and Martha play for about four hours. He isn't having a great night; when he leaves the table, he owes the casino a total of $4,500. He settles up with the cashier the next morning with a personal check on his Atlantic City bank account. His credit line will go back up only after his check clears his bank, a process that takes several days.

The following week, Dave is back in Atlantic City and Martha flies in from Montreal. Once again, they dine in one of the casino's restaurants and then head for the craps table. By now the casino waitresses know their preferences – Sancerre for the lady and a dirty martini for Mr. Z. –and bring them as soon as they take their regular place at the table. That night, Dave signs six markers, totaling $3,500. The next night he signs for another $2,000 in markers, and several more for $1,000 the third night. After a good winning streak, Dave makes up some of his losses, leaving his outstanding debt to the casino at $5,000.

Dave rapidly develops a routine: He generally stays in Atlantic City three or four days a week for business meetings and gambling, then returns home and divides his time between his offices in Elizabeth and Harrisburg. Louise loathes the casino and all that it represents; especially after years of living with boom-and-bust finances. She's always hated his gambling, but by now she's so accustomed to his constant trips to Atlantic City that she rarely raises the topic. She only comes to Atlantic City on special occasions or when Dave insists. However, he doesn't need to twist Martha's arm to get her to join him. She can't believe her luck in landing such a smart, successful and attractive man. She also loves the posh accommodations, the four-star comped restaurants, access to free salon services and the general pampering the casino's managers eagerly provide.

***

Dave has several affordable housing projects under development that urgently need his attention in Pennsylvania. So, he scales back his visits to Atlantic City to every one or two weeks. When he's in town, he works from his hotel suite during the day. When Martha's there, she often joins his business meetings. At night, they dine in a casino restaurant and shoot craps for a few hours. Dave doesn't like to eat alone, so when Martha's not around he generally invites one of his employees or consultants to have dinner with him. If Rich is in town, he always has dinner with Dave, even when Martha is there. Martha is the new business associate on the scene, but Rich is uneasy. He doesn't yet understand the blunt businesswoman or her role, or the intensity of Dave's gambling obsession, but doesn't question Dave about it.

One Monday evening, Steve Perskie and Dave meet for the first time over dinner at Dock's Oyster House, one of the oldest and most fashionable restaurants in Atlantic City, known for its well-connected, well-heeled clientele. Perskie is now a state senator. As he crosses the restaurant to reach their table, everybody in the place seems to know him and he pauses frequently to say hello and shake hands. Dave is impressed by Perskie's popularity and comes to realize that their meeting is long overdue. When Perskie reaches Dave's table the men shake hands and Perskie settles into his chair. He wastes little time on small talk.

"My phone has been ringing off the hook for weeks," he tells Dave. "Everyone is telling me, 'You gotta meet this Zarin guy. He can get affordable housing done'."

He grins at Dave. "How did you get known so quickly around here? You must be an incredible salesman."

After a few more minutes of small talk, Perskie says, "I assume you've met all the commissioners, including the mayor,"

Dave chooses his words carefully.

"Yes, and Mayor Lazarow seems to support housing."

Perskie leans forward slightly and lowers his voice. "I wouldn't be so sure of that," he cautions, quietly. "Lazarow will give you lip service, but I'm not so sure he'll step up when the time comes."

Dave looks at Perskie in surprise. Candor is rare from a politician.

"He's got limited vision," Perskie continues. "It's no help that in Atlantic City the commissioners, not the citizens, select the mayor. We're going to need to change that system to be more effective."

Perskie leans back, a smile returns to his face. "So, tell me, what's this product you're selling."

As Dave explains, Perskie listens carefully, but a look of doubt crosses his face. Spotting it, Dave pauses.

"I see a great unknown, though," Perskie says, again lowering his voice. "The casinos are so insular; I worry we'll end up with only a pocket of development along the casino corridor on the boardwalk. We originally drafted the legislation requiring the casinos to invest a meaningful percentage of their revenues in projects – like housing – to benefit the whole city. But it got watered down before passage, letting the casinos off the hook."

Perskie stops to allow a waiter to take their order. Once they're alone again, Perskie continues to explain Atlantic City's new realities to Dave.

"And now with the soaring land prices, affordable housing looks like a fantasy," Perskie says. Dave leans forward slightly and looks Perskie straight in the eye. Here, he thinks, is the right opening for his 'ask'.

"Steve, I have at least two housing projects coming together this year. If I can get them included in the next mortgage revenue bond financing by the New Jersey Housing Finance Agency, we may be able to get these projects going right away, *this* year."

He pauses for that to sink in.

"And I hear you're a good friend of William Johnston, the executive director of the agency. If you can make an introduction, I can make the case for him to include financing for the projects in this year's bond issue."

Perskie grins. "A salesman and a shrewd politician!" he says, tapping the table. "I like you, Dave. I'm impressed with what you're trying to accomplish. I can't promise anything, but I'll give Bill a call first thing tomorrow and encourage him to at least hear you out."

A few weeks later, on Tuesday, August 10, 1978, Dave and his team settle into their chairs at a large conference table at the offices of the New Jersey Housing Finance Agency. With Dave are Rich, Ken Smith, and his architect John Phillips. Executive Director William Johnston, a slightly balding, heavy-set man in his early 50s, and his team face Dave on the other side of the table. Dave launches into his pitch.

"I'm here to tell you about a number of housing projects we're planning."

"We've heard about you and know your reputation in building affordable housing," Johnston replies, smiling.

The members of Johnston's team nod in unison.

"Tell us what you have in mind," Johnston suggests. "We're all ears."

Dave gives Johnston a summary of his company's projects, starting with the fact that he built the first Section 8 housing project in the country in Allentown.

"We now have optioned several suitable sites in Atlantic City for building affordable housing." Dave pulls out a map of Atlantic City and spreads it across the table. He jabs his finger at one spot on the city's grid.

"We're thinking of a 175-unit Section 8 senior citizen project on Mediterranean Avenue and North Tennessee

Avenue. in the Northside of Atlantic City, where there's acute need for affordable housing." Dave turns to his architect, "John, tell our friends about the plans for this project."

John pulls out some preliminary architectural sketches showing an attractive 15-story brick building taking up the full block of Mediterranean Avenue. John goes into some detail about the quality of the building and the amenities that they plan to include.

Dave then turns to Ken. "Take us through the project costs and overall budget," he instructs him. Ken passes a copy of the financials to each of the officials and reviews the details with them.

Dave watches the officials intently, making sure they grasp all the nuances of Ken's presentation. Then it's back to him.

"We have a second project, and it's a little unusual," he says, attempting to pique their interest. It would involve the rehabilitation of three separate but nearby properties to create 153 units of affordable housing." Dave points to their locations.

"We've already acquired several Northside landmark properties, including the Liberty Hotel, the Northside YMCA and the former Illinois Avenue schoolhouse. We intend to rehabilitate these buildings." Once again, Dave turns to his staff, calling on them to explain the design and financials.

Johnston is clearly impressed. "Dave, you've done a lot of work in a short period of time. What exactly do you need from us?" Dave directs a steady gaze at Johnston.

"To move forward, we need an $8 million low-interest loan from your agency for the first project, and a $6.7 million low-interest loan to make the second project a reality."

Johnston pauses, and purses his lip thoughtfully. "That's something we could consider for next year—"

"Not next year," Dave cuts in. "The community needs affordable housing now; in fact, they needed it yesterday. You have a multi-family, Section 8 assisted tax-exempt housing bond issue going out this October. We need these projects included in this year's bond offering." Johnston's eyes widen at Dave's brashness.

"Mr. Zarin, we are issuing that bond in just two months!" Johnston is incredulous; a tone of irritation creeps into his voice. "The prospectus is nearly complete. I don't see how we can make these changes at this late date."

Dave sits up in his chair and leans forward calmly.

"Mr. Johnston, the casino referendum passed in 1976," he says quietly. "This law was intended to give Atlantic City a new lease on life. It's now 1978. The first casino is open, and many more are going up. Yet there isn't a single new housing project anywhere in the city underway or even in the pipeline. And certainly not any new affordable housing. We have two projects ready to go."

The timing of the financing is critical for Dave, and he's pulling out all the stops to convince Johnston to move quickly.

"Senator Perskie and Governor Byrne are watching and getting impatient for Atlantic City to meet the needs of its citizens. So is the rest of the city and State – and the country. Further delay won't reflect well on your agency or the city."

Johnston is nodding, albeit reluctantly.

"The Black community is already very skeptical of the govern-ment's commitment to them," Dave adds. "If we don't get put on this bond issue in October, we may not get funding for these projects until next year at the earliest," Dave dials back the tone of urgency in his remark.

"And that means we can't break ground until late next year. That's three years after the law was passed."

Dave launches his final pitch by offering a carrot.

"If these projects get into this bond issue, Senator Perskie, Governor Byrne and you can get great PR about these new affordable housing projects. And we can get started early next year."

Dave sits back in his seat. His eyes are still riveted to Johnston's face. "What will it be, Mr. Johnston?"

Johnston feels a knot in his stomach. He's loath to become the target of the governor's displeasure and receive a hectoring phone call from his office. Dave has pushed exactly the right buttons.

Johnston turns to his finance chief.

"Matt, can we do this?"

Matt pauses and looks upward in thought. "If we increase the amount of the offering by several million dollars, we may be able to pull it off. So long as the board okays it."

Johnston exhales, then turns to Dave. "We'll do our best," he says with a sigh.

As Dave had expected, the New Jersey Housing Finance Board approves the additional money in the bond issue slated for sale later that year. The stars are aligning in favor of Dave's first Atlantic City projects – at least when it comes to the financing. But he wants to ensure he has the community's support before moving forward. In the coming months, as Dave continues to manage his various projects, he quietly lobbies various business groups and community organizations in Atlantic City to support the creation of affordable housing. Likewise, he continues to work with Pierre to build trust with elected officials, especially the city commissioners.

With his characteristic attention to detail, Dave is focused on ensuring that his projects sail through various zoning reviews and government approvals. He knows he still has work to do, and gets started.

***

In July, Dave and Martha return to Atlantic City and the craps table. His credit balance now stands at $5,000 – half of what he started with. Dave then has a good run, winning over $3,000. He hands the chips in a tray to Martha.

"Here, take these over to the cashier and pick up markers for the same amount." Martha isn't used to being a gofer, but she doesn't mind. She loves holding thousands of dollars in chips in her hands. As she crosses the casino floor, servers and casino security guards greet her, "How's it going, Mrs. Z?"

As Martha hands over the chips, the cage manager jokes with her like they're pals.

"Is this all the chips you are cashing?" he teases. "I expected more from you and Mr. Z."

Meanwhile, Dave is still gambling. By the time she gets back to the table, he's losing steadily, and signs six more markers for $1,000 each. Although he has just redeemed $3,000 in markers, Dave hits his $10,000 credit limit. Irked by what he sees as an arbitrary cap on his gambling, Dave heads upstairs, as Martha pats his arm reassuringly.

"Don't worry. Let's talk to them about it tomorrow," she says, brightly.

The next evening, Dave asks Randy Mihelic, the casino's assistant credit manager, to raise his credit limit. Randy readily agrees and boosts the limit to $12,000. Dave immediately heads to the craps table and requests a marker for $2,000. The boxman hesitates, knowing that Dave hit his $10,000 limit the day before. He looks over to the pit boss, who gives him a nod. The dealer hands Dave $25 and $100 chips totaling $2,000.

As usual, Dave gives Martha $100 worth of $25 chips. In fifteen minutes of play, Dave presses his bets three times before taking any winnings off the table. He's on a solid winning streak. When the shooter finally sevens-out, Dave has won more than $7,500. Elated, he keeps playing, but his luck sours again. After signing four more markers, he once again has hit his credit limit. The only difference? He now owes Resorts $12,000 instead of $10,000.

He leaves the craps table with only two $25 chips, walks over to the cage, and writes a personal check for $12,000. That's the only way he'll be able to play here again.

Readying for bed in Dave's room, as she unwraps her silk robe, Martha asks him why he likes to gamble so much.

"When I am playing craps, I don't think about anything else. It takes my mind completely off work and relieves the constant pressure and stress I feel. I can relax," he explains. "Nothing compares with the excitement of gambling."

"When you get into a rhythm, when luck comes over to your side, it's exhilarating," Dave continues, growing animated. "It's better than sex!"

Martha stiffens at the perceived insult. Furious, she climbs silently into bed and turns her back to Dave.

Days later, noting his substantial gambling activity, the casino moves Dave into a larger three-room suite with a small but fully-equipped kitchen and formal dining table, a large living room with plush, dove gray leather couches and rosewood end tables, and a spacious master bedroom. On her next visit to Atlantic City, Martha is thrilled by the new accommodations.

"Wow," she coos upon entering his suite. "What a divine upgrade, Dave!" She strokes the sofa's soft Italian leather. Martha isn't shy about asking for perks for herself, either, and is making the most of her VIP status at the casino and hotel boutiques selling designer clothes and shoes.

When the staff call her "Mrs. Z.", she doesn't correct them. Sure, Martha wants Dave to leave Louise. But she isn't pushing it. Martha already has him – and his high-roller lifestyle –most of the time anyway. Louise is out of the way "probably baking cookies in Elizabeth," Martha tells her sister, snickering. It's a cozy arrangement.

Over the next several months Dave intensifies his juggling act, as he spends his days managing multiple development projects and his evenings escalating his gambling. Resorts raises Dave's credit limit again, initially to $20,000 and then, only six days later, to $25,000. Equally rapidly, Dave exhausts his available credit, and writes a personal check for $25,000 in return for his markers. Two weeks later, in September, the casino raises his limit yet again, to $30,000, a figure that Dave reaches only two days later. He writes a personal check for this amount on September 16. At this point, it seems as if Dave and Resorts are locked in a financial arms race: The higher the casino raises his credit, the more he gambles – and loses.

On September 30, he cashes in a promissory note of $1.1 million at his local bank in Elizabeth from one of his Pennsylvania housing projects payable to his company next year. He begins borrowing from his company's funds to pay off his gambling losses at Resorts.

The casino is nothing but accommodating. It boosts his limit to $35,000 on October 1. Dave is now playing for such high stakes that the hotel assigns him a safe deposit box at the front desk to provide him with a place where he can put his winnings if he has a good night. Even so, the casino seems to be winning the betting race; Dave's losses continue to mount. Cash rarely ends up in the safe deposit box.

At about this time, Dave attracts the attention of the senior officers at Resorts, including Steve Norton, vice president of hotel operations, Jack Davis, president of Resorts, and James Crosby, the company's chairman. Dave's credit rating is still only at 2; he hasn't reached the elite status of being a 1. But the hours he devotes to the craps table virtually every night he is in town, his flamboyance at the table, and the steadily increasing size of his bets has players and staff abuzz. Jim Carr, the casino's vice president of operations, monitors their VIP gambler's activity on a weekly basis. They want to keep him happy.

On October 6, Carr stops Dave and Martha on their way to the craps table.

"Dave, I have good news about your credit," he tells the couple. "We know you dislike our limits and the delays in resetting you're limits until your checks clear through the banking system and get deposited in our account."

"We know your payment history and that your checks are always good, so from now on we'll consider your checks cleared as soon as we deposit them at our bank the next morning."

From now on, Dave won't face the kind of delay imposed on most gamblers when he hits his limit. "You're a great customer and we want to do our best to take care of you," Carr adds.

As Dave thanks him, Martha adds her own perspective to the conversation.

"Well, I'm glad you've realized this! We've been giving Resorts a lot of business!" she exclaims. "Even if Dave doesn't always notice, I see how he creates a lot of excitement that draws other players to the tables. That has to be worth something tangible."

Both Jim and Dave stare at Martha in surprise for several seconds. Stepping back slightly, Jim looks at Dave.

"Well, like I said Dave, we appreciate your business and want to be of service." He nods curtly to Martha and walks away.

Although Martha's bluntness makes Dave wince at the time, he comes to appreciate the truth of her remarks to Carr as he replays them in his head. He chafes at the credit limits the casino imposes on him. Over breakfast at the end of October, Dave tells Martha he's still frustrated with the credit limits Resorts imposes on him.

"It disrupts my betting strategy and keeps me from winning," he grouses. He falls silent, frowning.

Suddenly his face lights up. "Martha, there's a way around that. Would you be willing to open a credit line that I can use to gamble? Of course, I'll write personal checks to you to cover any outstanding markers on your account." He adds what he hopes will be the clincher. "I think that will help turn around my luck."

Martha sips her coffee and ponders his request. Over the last six months during her visits to Atlantic City, she and Dave have been almost joined at the hip. From their first night together in Miami, Martha's been smitten with Dave. She's waited to declare her feelings. Now's the time, she decides.

"Dave, I would do anything for you," she says. "I interrupt my work to fly down here, sometimes at my own expense, because you want me to. Night after night I'm with you at the craps table putting up with the noise and cigarette smoke."

She pauses several seconds.

"I do that because I love you."

Dave's reaction isn't what she's hoping for.

"Look, Martha, you mean a lot to me," he says softly, lowering his eyes. "I deeply respect you and admire your business savvy and confidence – I find it sexy. For now, let's just keep our relationship as it is."

Martha grudgingly accepts this. She has met Dave's family and knows his family entanglements are keeping him from leaving his wife. "It's complicated," she often tells her sister. Years in real estate have taught her patience and the importance of playing a long game. Martha is convinced he'll come around – to her.

She puts her cards on the table. "Dave, that doesn't change how I feel about you." She's disappointed, yet still, she loves him.

"About opening a credit line, I have certificates of deposit at two banks in Montreal, and use those CDs as security for lines of credit at the banks," she tells Dave. "If you write me your personal checks to cover any markers I need to pay off, I don't see why I couldn't do that. How much should I ask for?"

Dave's elated. "Let's start at $25,000," he says immediately.

That evening, Dave and Martha stop by the cashier's cage and Martha's application for a $25,000 credit line is approved. At the craps table, Dave signs a marker for $2,000. After the dealer hands Dave his chips, Martha also asks to sign a marker for $2,000. The dealer counts out $2,000 in chips and reaches across the table to her.

Martha holds up her hand, "Please give these chips to Mr. Z." she says. The dealer smoothly slides the chips to Dave. They continue to gamble for over three hours.

Weeks later, Dave has a new credit limit of $50,000 and hits it in early November. The very next day Dave also exhausts Martha's new credit limit of $35,000. He then cashes a non-gaming check for $5,000 at the hotel's front desk, a personal check which is supposed to be used for nominal personal or business needs such as carfare, not for gambling. He uses that money to gamble that night. A few days later Dave writes a check to buy back all his outstanding markers, and Martha's as well. They're all paid up, with a clean slate. For the moment.

Later in November and into December, Dave begins winning substantial money at craps: over $100,000 in November and $60,000 in December. But no matter how much he wins, he loses more. And as the days pass his losses continue to mount. Dave asks Martha to use a personal check on her account to buy back his markers so he can continue to use his credit line to gamble.

As these events are unfolding, I'm living and working in New York and go down to Atlantic City on occasion. I enjoy the full VIP treatment that Resorts extends to Dave's family: a comped hotel room, free meals and drinks. In the casino, Dave often gives me one or two $100 chips to go off and gamble. (If I win, I keep the winnings and return the chips to him.)

After months of watching Dave playing craps, my brother Rich and I are increasingly concerned about gambling's grip on Dave, not to mention Martha's hold over him, too. Eventually, I confront Dave about the sizable bets he's making at the table. He waves me off:

"This is my form of entertainment. It relaxes me and lets me blow off steam," he tells me. "I know what I'm doing, it's my money, and I can afford it."

Then comes his final point, soon to be a constant refrain: "I have it under control."

And then, there's Martha. Rich and I both dislike her sense of entitlement, how Dave seems to tolerate Martha's voracious appetite for perks and comps. What's more, in her interactions with Dave, she clearly behaves more like a wife than a business associate. On several occasions, I ask Dave point blank if they're having an affair.

Each time, he shrugs and ducks the question, and avoids making eye contact.

"She's just a business associate," he replies. "Nothing more."

These glib responses, together with Martha's overbearing person-ality, only make it more clear to us that he is having an affair. Rich and I are increasingly uneasy about the combustible combination of Dave's gambling fixation and Martha's apparent grip over him.

It's early December when Gary Grant joins the casino as the new credit manager. He introduces himself to Dave over coffee just off the casino floor.

"You're the talk of the casino," Gary says.

"Well, I hope it's all good things," Dave replies with a chuckle.

Gary is quick to reassure him.

"Oh yes, you've got a great reputation and we value you as a customer. What can we do to keep you a *happy* customer?"

Dave answers instantly.

"Get rid of the credit limit. It restricts my playing." He recites his credentials as a successful entrepreneur. "In Atlantic City, we have several housing projects under development. So, give me a break on the credit limit. It's keeping me from winning."

Gary thinks for a moment.

"We'll do what we can about that, Dave." He places his hands on the table. "For now, feel free to use one of our limos whenever you need it, like traveling back and forth from Elizabeth to Atlantic City."

Gary is right: Dave does have a terrific reputation with everyone, including politicians, community leaders and businessmen across Atlantic City. The brash developer from North Jersey is getting known as a dynamic mover and shaker. Dave works to maintain good relationships with the mayor and each city commissioner, and strengthens his alliance with State Senator Perskie.

He also seizes every chance to make his case directly to grass-roots community organizations and neighborhoods. He's particularly close to Pierre, who invites him to speak at the December meeting of the local chapter of the NAACP. More than 70 people turn out for the meeting at the Presbyterian Church on Arctic Avenue. They include some of the Black community's most influential leaders: James Usry, the deputy superintendent of schools (and a future mayor), and Barbara Woodall, the head of community affairs for Atlantic City.

Pierre introduces Dave with high praise.

"We've all seen smiley, fast-talking developers come through town before, spouting off all kinds of promises," he reminds the audience. "All were empty promises. None ever resulted in affordable housing actually getting built in our neighborhood." Dave, he tells them, is different.

"I've come to know Dave over many months. He's the real deal. He wants to build low- and middle-income and senior citizen housing in the Northside and elsewhere in the city. I want you to meet him and to judge him for yourself. If we want him to get things done, he'll need our full support. He's here to ask you himself."

Pierre nods to Dave, sitting alongside him on the dais.

Dave takes the microphone and launches into his usual pitch, describing his background and the projects he's successfully completed. He tells the audience that he plans to bring the same expertise – and results – to Atlantic City's most blighted areas.

"It's just a beginning. It's real. It's coming. But, of course, it barely scratches the surface of what needs to be done in the community. Any renaissance in Atlantic City needs to help the people who live here. Affordable housing is a key component of this rebirth."

Several members of the audience murmur in approval and exchange nods with each other. Some even clap.

Dave holds up his hand. "Please understand that I'm not doing this work for altruistic reasons. I intend to make a profit on these housing projects. But, at the same time, I'm not doing these projects *just* for the money."

He describes building affordable housing as his life's mission. It's "a small contribution to address a very great need. With your help and support, we can succeed." The audience breaks into applause. Dave has totally won them over, sold them on his character and on the specifics of his proposal.

A few months later, Dave attends a hearing seeking the Atlantic City Planning Board's approval for the Liberty Apartments (formerly, the Liberty Hotel), the Disston Apartments (formerly, the YMCA), and the Schoolhouse Apartments (formerly, the Illinois Avenue schoolhouse) in Northside. Dave has ensured that the room is packed with his supporters. After Dave's team makes its presentation and answers questions from board members, the hearing then opens for public comment. Barbara Woodall, the community organizer for Atlantic City, a tall Black woman with an engaging smile and commanding personality, speaks passionately about the need for affordable housing in the Northside and the importance to the community of rehabilitating these historical properties and converting them to housing. A senior member of the local chapter of the NAACP also speaks in favor of the project. Several labor unions, including the head of the Painter's Union, also voice their support. There's no public opposition. The vote to approve Dave's projects is unanimous.

***

Things aren't going as smoothly for Dave at the craps table. By the end of 1978, Dave owes Martha a steadily-increasing amount of money for the personal checks she is writing to redeem his markers. Sitting in her comped hotel room one afternoon near the end of December, Martha adds up how much she has paid out to Resorts for Dave's markers, then she makes a list of the checks she's written for which Dave still hasn't reimbursed her. When she sees the total – $200,000 – she gasps in alarm.

A substantial sum like that is enough to make her question the entire arrangement with Dave. Initially, she wanted to help the man she loved. But this has become something altogether different. The realization strikes her: For Dave, she comes second to gambling. Does this mean he cares more about the money she lends to him than he does about her? Filled with doubt and anxiety, Martha hurries to Dave's suite and walks in. She doesn't notice he's in the middle of a staff meeting.

"We have to talk," she says, her voice shaking. Non-plussed, Dave stares at her. "*Now.*"

She pulls Dave into the bedroom, closing the door behind them, shutting out his shocked staff.

"I've just done the math and found that you still owe me $200,000 to cover personal checks I wrote to the casino on your behalf," she says. Her mouth tightens into a straight line.

"What are you going to do about it? I need you to make me whole."

Dave reddens, more out of anger at her tone than embarrassment at the situation.

"You know I'm good for it, Martha," he tells her sharply. "I need all of my available cash to play craps and to keep my credit limit down." He asks her to be patient.

"We've got a lot of projects under development. I'll be able to pay you back as they move forward. Okay?"

Martha studies Dave for a moment, considering his answer. Dave shifts his feet; glances at the door. He needs to get back to his meeting. She calms down a little. But his stinging remark that gambling is "better than sex!" still echoes in Martha's head. She hardens her face and her voice.

"Dave, I need something on paper," she tells him, icily. "I need to feel comfortable and to not have to worry about this."

Dave offers her a compromise. "How about if I give you a promissory note for these monies?"

Martha shoots back. "I'm losing a lot of interest on this money. What about *that*?" Her voice is rising, prompting Dave to glance again at the door, this time in anxiety.

"OK, OK, Martha," he says soothingly. "What can I do to make you happy?" Dave is oblivious to the irony of using the precise words that Gary Grant used with him only days earlier.

Martha's demand is simple. "Pay me weekly interest on what you owe until it's all repaid."

"Okay," Dave replies, slowly. "How much interest do you want?"

"A thousand dollars a week."

Dave gasps as he quickly runs the numbers in his head. $1,000 a week in interest on a $200,000 one-year loan comes to more than 25 percent interest. "But loan sharks don't charge that high an interest rate!" he protests.

Martha shrugs. She isn't budging. Dave passes his hand through his hair in frustration. "Okay, Martha. I'll ask my attorney to prepare a promissory note for me to sign."

CHAPTER 6: COMPS AND CREDIT

Even as Martha pressures Dave to repay what he owes to her, Dave continues to gamble, usually with Martha at his side. Dave once again hits his credit limit, which by now is $50,000, and reaches Martha's limit of $35,000 as well.

He writes a personal check for $30,000 at the cashier's cage and picks up markers for this amount. When Dave resumes his usual place at the craps table, his credit balance is $20,000. He settles in for a few hours of gambling and hits a hot winning streak. A crowd gathers around the table, once again buzzing excitedly about Mr. Z's boldness and luck. He has bets on all of the numbers, and wins. He presses his bet for the next roll, then again, and once again.

The cheers are louder with each roll. But Martha isn't cheering. By now she knows how this will end and thinks pressing a bet when you're ahead is stupid. The shooter continues without "sevening-out" for more than 15 minutes. Dave is ecstatic. He's up $10,000 when his luck changes again. He presses his bets and loses again and again on seven-outs.

Martha, standing beside him, is increasingly anxious as she sees the winnings evaporate.

"Why don't you take some of the money, rather than continually pressing your bets?" she snaps at him. The other players, as well as the dealers, stop and stare at the couple.

"You're a jack of all trades and a master of none. Let me gamble my own way," Dave snaps back.

The stickman, suppressing a smile, immediately slides the dice over to the shooter as if nothing has happened. The shooter tosses a seven, and Dave loses, again.

Over the next few hours, Dave signs six markers of $5,000 each. Once again, he bumps up against his credit limit and now owes the casino a total of $85,000 (including Martha's limit). The same night the pit boss finally raises Dave's gambler rating to a 1. He's heavily in debt, sure – but he's now officially part of the gambling world's elite.

A few days later Gary Grant seeks out Dave and Martha to tell them that Resorts will now also consider Martha's personal checks from her banks in Montreal as cleared as soon as Resorts deposits them into its bank account the next morning. Until now, that process has taken six to eight weeks for a check drawn on Martha's Canadian bank account to clear.

"Expediting the process for Martha's checks should help you with the credit limit." Gary seems pleased with his creative work-around. But Martha is indignant that this hasn't been standard procedure all along.

"When I write a check, it's like cash. It is paid," she says caustically.

Dave registers Gary's shock and shakes his head at the casino exec in silent apology.

Taking Martha by the elbow, Dave steers her back to the craps table.

"Look Martha," he says to her tightly, "Gary's a good guy to both of us, let's not bite the hand that feeds us, okay?"

In April the casino is abuzz with excitement: Frank Sinatra and Sammy Davis Jr. will appear at the hotel's 1500-seat Superstar Theater. Tickets are so hard to get that even top Atlantic City politicians can't get in. Dave and Louise are big fans of both crooners, so Resorts arranges for them to sit on the banquette overlooking the packed theater. Rich and his wife Susan, as well as Ken Smith and his wife sit with them.

Resorts seats Martha on the banquette, too, at the far end of the table from Dave and his family. Martha glares at Louise and Dave throughout the evening, as Frank and Sammy sing 16 songs. Sinatra sings his signature "New York, New York," and ends the show with the gambler's anthem, "Luck be a Lady." It's a memorable, bittersweet evening that reminds Louise of happier times with Dave.

Two weeks later, Gary tells Dave and Martha that senior management will move him into the Frank Sinatra suite – their premier accommodations. "It's for your use exclusively whenever you are here, unless Sinatra is in town to perform. It's our expression of appreciation and gratitude for your business."

"Well, I'm glad to see that the hotel is finally recogniz- ing what a great and valuable customer Dave is," Martha blurts out. "Other boardwalk casinos are opening shortly and you should want to do whatever you can to keep Dave coming back to Resorts." Martha pauses briefly, then adds: "I'd like a room adjacent to the Sinatra suite."

Gary looks at Martha, a bit aghast. Dave, visibly irritated by Martha's rudeness, remains silent. Gary takes his cue from Mr. Z, his biggest VIP.

"Sure, Martha," Gary says silkily without missing a beat. "No problem."

The Sinatra suite is stunningly garish, even by 1970s standards. Martha is jubilant about the status the two-bedroom suite conveys on them. It's strictly for VVIPs, like Dave. It features a fully equipped kitchen and huge living room with a sofa and chairs in red butter-soft leather and burnt-orange shag carpeting.

Floor-to-ceiling windows offer panoramic views of the boardwalk and ocean. A baby grand piano sits near a fully stocked bar and a large brass dining table and chairs. Adding to the glitz is a crystal chandelier sparkling in the sunlight flooding through the windows. The enormous master bed-room boasts a king-sized bed, an oversized bathroom and a walk-in closet large enough for a full-size craps table.

Dave is spending more and more of his time in Atlantic City, and uses the suite for meetings with local politicians, business leaders, business partners and government officials. Gary places the Resorts limousine at Dave's disposal full time. The car ferries him to and from the casino to his home or offices and transports Martha to and from Philadelphia airport, 90 minutes away, when she comes to town.

***

Dave enjoys holding his business meetings at the suite, where he feels he gets a home-field advantage in deal making. Today he's considering two property lots totaling four acres on the corner of North Carolina and Huron Avenue near the Marina area where casinos are to be built. The land is expensive; it won't be profitable to use it as a site for affordable housing. Dave believes it's a good spot for high-rise market rental units and a marina.

But the land owner, Ed Simms, has an aggressive and difficult personality. Short, overweight and in his 50s,

Simms owns a construction excavation company and recently pocketed millions from the sale of other property to a casino developing a new venture. Dave's consultant says Simms wants $2.5 million for the land. That's way too much for Dave. So, he invites Simms to meet with him and Ken, his project manager, in the Sinatra suite.

After Simms and his associate arrive, Dave watches them absorb all the details of the lavish room. The two men make small talk while sizing each other up. Once again, Dave explains his myriad affordable housing projects, suggesting that he wants Simms' parcel for a similar venture.

"So, Ed," Dave plunges into the heart of the matter, "I understand we're at an impasse on the price. As you know, I can't pay a lot for this property. It would make it impossible for us to build affordable housing. The rental rates wouldn't cover the mortgage,"

Simms isn't buying it.

"Dave, everybody knows you're getting cheap money from the Housing Finance Agency. I don't think the price is really a problem." Simms glances around the suite appraisingly.

"I'm sure you can entice Resorts or another casino to put up low-interest financing for your projects."

Dave rolls his eyes dismissively.

"Nice thought, but the real world doesn't work that way," he retorts.

The men haggle for another twenty minutes and both begin to lose patience. Their voices grow louder.

"I can afford to pay at most $1.2 million. That is as high as I can go," Dave says, by now utterly exasperated.

"Two million. That's my best price," Simms shoots back.

Dave spends a minute digesting that counteroffer. Suddenly, he bolts out of his chair and crosses the floor to tower over the still-seated Simms.

"I've had it," he yells into Simms' upturned face. "I'm done. Go fuck a monkey."

Dave then grabs Ken by the arm, pulls him into the master bedroom and slams the door. Sitting down on the bed, he exhales slowly, and smirks at Ken. "Oh well, sometimes you gotta do that."

Back in the main room, sitting in view of the piano that Frank Sinatra – Sinatra! – plays whenever he comes to town, Simms is in shock. He glances over at his partner; both men are unsure whether the meeting is over. They sit silently for another five minutes, then get up and leave.

But the haggling isn't over: Dave's real estate broker and Simms resume the negotiations on the phone over the next several days and eventually agree on a price of $1.35 million for the property. That's far less than Simms' "best price" at the meeting in the Sinatra suite. Dave's calculated tantrum, another high-risk bet, pays off.

***

Dave and Martha are again at their usual spot at the craps table. After only two hours of play, Dave has hit his $50,000 credit limit *and* exhausted Martha's. He has only $200 in chips left. When he asks the dealer to sign another marker for $5,000, the pit boss walks over, telling him quietly that he has no more credit available.

Visibly upset, Dave stalks to Gary Grant, who is standing at the cashier's cage.

"Gary, why do you keep imposing credit limits on me and interrupting my play?" Dave demands. "You know I can afford to do what I'm doing,"

Dave's face is flushed in anger. "You know I've *always* paid any outstanding gambling debt. I need my credit limit raised. Now."

Gary is taken aback by Dave's aggression.

"All right Dave, I'll tell you what I can do," he says quietly, hoping to ease the tension. "I'll TTO you for $30,000."

"What do you mean TTO?" he asks in confusion.

Gary explains that the acronym stands for 'This Trip Only'.

"I can raise your limit temporarily above the credit line, usually for one night or at most for several days, until you leave town," Gary says.

"This permits you to gamble beyond your credit line, up to an extra $30,000. But at the end of the limited TTO period, if you owe more than your regular credit limit, you'll need to give us a personal check to bring your credit balance back down to that point."

Casino policy governing TTOs is very loose. The credit manager has no restrictions on the amount of TTO credit he can give a patron. Nor does the casino limit the number of times he can extend that TTO to a customer on the same night. All the crucial decisions are in the hands of the credit manager – in this case, Gary Grant. He can therefore allow a player to keep gambling indefinitely. It makes the concept of a credit ceiling almost meaningless.

Gary's offer placates Dave. "OK, that works for me," he says calmly.

Gary accompanies him back to the pit boss overseeing Dave's craps table.

"Jack, I just TTO'd Mr. Z for $30,000," Gary tells him. Jack nods.

Dave rejoins Martha and resumes playing – and losing. By the following night he's reached his TTO limit of $80,000, and writes a personal check to the casino for $50,000. Later that month, the casino raises Dave's credit limit to $100,000.

Dave's financial juggling act intensifies. Several weeks later, he borrows $420,000 from one of his business partners on the West Coast, promising to repay the loan from progress payments due to Dave on several of his projects. Shortly thereafter, he borrows $215,000 from the Guarantee National Bank in Atlantic City, putting up as collateral certain promissory notes payable to Dave's company from the sale of two Pennsylvania housing projects. Martha also continues to lend money to Dave to fuel his gambling. He now owes her another $200,000, and writes her a second promissory note for that amount.

On June 6, 1979, Dave asks Gary Grant if he can cash a non-gaming check at the cashier's cage. He needs the cash to meet his payroll, he explains. Gray agrees to accommodate his VIP. Dave cashes a personal check for $50,000 and takes the money up to his suite. Two hours later, Dave returns to the craps table. He loses all the money.

As all this is unfolding, I'm in the middle of the Pacific, working as a young lawyer with the government of the island of Palau as it negotiates a change in sovereignty status with the United States. Midway through June 1979, I return home for two weeks, accompanying Palau's official delegation. My girlfriend and I had gotten engaged in Palau and decide to get married during this trip back to the U.S. I ask my mother to arrange a small wedding but make clear that I don't want Martha to be invited. In my eyes, she's anything but a member of our family.

Martha, who by now considers herself a close family friend – at the very least – is furious and takes it out on Dave.

"Your son," she hisses at him, "Is trying to break us up!"

When Dave ignores her words. Martha reminds him of the large IOUs to her. "I loaned you a lot of money, Dave, and you owe me," she argues fiercely. "You have to tell your son to include me."

When my fiancée and I arrive at Kennedy Airport in New York, we take a taxi to the Carnegie Deli where we plan to meet my brother. I had been dreaming about noshing on New York's deli food for the past six months. But almost as soon as we're seated around the table, Rich delivers a bombshell.

"There's a glitch in your wedding plans," he warns me. "Dad is really pissed that you won't invite Martha to the wedding. He says he won't attend unless you invite Martha."

I am disappointed, but not surprised; I've seen Martha's hold on Dave.

"Well, I hope he changes his mind and decides to come," I tell Rich. "But she's still not invited."

Rich doesn't like confrontation and looks uncomfortable about potential conflict between me and Dave. But he doesn't argue. From there, our conversation takes what seems to be an inevitable turn.

"What's happening with Dad's gambling?" I ask Rich. "Has anything changed since I left the country?"

Rich grimaces.

"Mom's really worried, but doesn't talk about it," he tells me. "Dad's spending more and more time in Atlantic City and gambles almost every night for hours on end. His bets are getting bigger and riskier."

Rich pauses, scowling.

"And Martha seems to be egging him on. I think she's loaned him money. But who knows? Dad isn't talking about it."

Rich sighs.

"Every time you raise the gambling issue with him, he shuts you down. He keeps saying, 'I am in control' of the gambling."

"So Rich, *is* he in control?" I ask.

"I just don't know," Rich confesses. "I don't know what to do, because it's starting to divert his attention from business. You know Dad, he never loses track over the smallest detail, always full of questions, and meticulous on follow up. But now, it's like he's left everything to his staff. He's just not himself."

For the first time, we consider the possibility that he'll end up losing all the money he is making from his projects. It's like we're watching a train wreck in slow motion, but can't do anything to stop it.

"Imagine working hard all those years building his business, only to lose it all at the craps table," Rich says in frustration and fury.

I couldn't agree more.

"How sad is that?" I add.

Despite Martha's demand and angry outbursts, Dave attends my wedding without her.

By the time I fly back to Palau accompanied by my new wife, Atlantic City's second casino opens its doors with great fanfare. Making its debut on June 26, 1979, the Boardwalk Regency Hotel and Casino occupies the former site of an old Howard Johnson's. Owned by the Caesars World Corporation, it's now the largest casino in the world. Although the casino isn't officially called Caesars, everyone refers to it as such.

Martha has come a long way from her initial wariness about gambling. Now, she pushes Dave to try out the new casino and persuades him to fill out a credit application to play craps. When Caesars checks on Dave's credit history with other casinos, the news rockets up the Resorts' chain of command. Casino executives scramble to come up with new enticements to keep him gambling at *their* tables.

Six weeks later, in early August, Dave and Martha venture out to the Boardwalk Regency to gamble. Caesars executives start Dave with a credit line of $50,000. He and Martha hope a change in venue will change his luck. It doesn't. He uses up most of his credit line during the next few evenings.

Meanwhile, at Resorts, on her way to the spa for her weekly massage, Martha buttonholes Gary Grant to tell him they've been gambling at Caesars.

"They're very pleased to have Dave at their tables, " Martha says. "As a friend, Gary, I'm just letting you know you'll have to do more for us If you want to keep him coming back."

***

In between his gambling stints, Dave pushes forward with plans to build more housing for Atlantic City. It's late August 1979, and Dave needs to nail down zoning approval to build the New York Avenue Apartments, a 150-unit high-rise Section 8 apartment building for seniors.

In an effort to line up support for his application, he meets with Mayor Joe Lazarow at his City Hall office to discuss the project. Although Lazarow, an Atlantic City native, has been under fire in the press for his administration's lack of initiative on affordable housing, he is – at best – a reluctant supporter of Dave's projects. As a result, the relationship between Dave and Lazarow is strained. Behind his oversized desk, Lazarow isn't smiling. He sees Dave as a pushy outsider – from North Jersey, no less.

The dislike is mutual: Dave thinks Lazarow is inept, and that he looks like a squat garden gnome. Still, Dave sets aside his antipathy to explain the zoning approvals he's seeking. Lazarow interrupts several times to point out obstacles that will hold up the process. Dave is prepared for that and in turn offers a solution to each issue. A frustrated and irritable Lazarow finally loses his cool.

"What's a nice Jewish boy like you building houses for the *shvartzas*?" he blurts out, using a Yiddish pejorative for Black people.

Dave sits stock still for a moment, then silently rises from his chair and walks to the door.

He turns back to face Lazarow.

"If you don't support this project, your press criticism is going to get a lot worse. I'll make sure of it."

Dave then walks out.

***

Meanwhile, Resorts executives heed Martha's none-too-subtle warning and, alarmed at the prospect of losing Dave's business to a rival, they raise his credit limit to $150,000. Now, midway through August, he has already drawn on $130,000. Dave and Martha are back at their usual spot at the craps table in Resorts, and Dave signs a marker for $5,000. When the stickman slides the dice to a new shooter, Dave keeps increasing the size of his wagers, pressing his bets in his usual manner. He signs two additional $5,000 markers, then a $3,000 marker and finally a $2,000 marker that evening, reaching his credit limit. That same month, Dave cashes four non-gaming checks and uses the money from each to gamble.

That same month, Gary Grant and Dave meet up over coffee. As usual, they chat about developments in Atlantic City and exchange scuttlebutt about business and politics. Then the conversation turns to Dave's gambling. Gary has been watching Dave's obsessive play for months with growing concern.

"Dave, I'm telling you as a friend, I think you need to slow down your gambling and take it easy for a while. You need to relax, do something else."

But Dave isn't willing to even entertain the possibility of slowing down. "I am at a certain age in my life where I've made my own money, where I am now an extremely wealthy man, and if I want to shoot craps with my money," Dave says, curtly. "it's my business."

Dave thinks that should be the last word on the subject but Gary presses him further.

"Dave, your low-income housing projects are essential for the future of our city," he says. "You talk about your meetings with state and local officials. You need to understand that the casino keeps records, including about you, that are an open book," Gary says in a low voice.

"If the Division of Gaming Enforcement or the Casino Control Commission wants to look at these records, they'll have access to them. You're here a lot, you're the biggest player in town." He adds. "I don't know if these two things are compatible."

Dave shakes his head.

"Don't worry Gary," Dave says, and the repeats his mantra: "I have it under control."

Dave stands up and adds, "But I appreciate your input." He heads straight back to the craps table.

***

Throughout college and law school, my childhood neighbor and traveling buddy Jon Epstein and I remain friends. He also stays in touch with Dave through college and law school. When my father goes to the Garden State Racetrack in Cherry Hill, he often calls Jon, who by now finished law school and lives nearby, to join him. After Jon passes the bar exam, he spends several years working at

Legal Aid before opening a solo law practice in the Spring 1979. With a freshly-painted shingle outside his office, Jon now needs clients, and Dave presents one of his best opportunities. At this point, seven years following the company's near-death experience, Dave's business is thriving, not just surviving. He's got lots of housing projects underway, in Atlantic City and elsewhere.

Just before Labor Day weekend, Jon calls Dave. He opens their phone chat with warm pleasantries, then asks Dave if he and his girlfriend might accompany Dave on their next racetrack trip.

"Sure, Louise and I will be spending Saturday morning at the Long Beach Club before heading to Monmouth Racetrack," Dave says. "Why don't you meet us at the club and we can go to the track from there?"

The club offers its affluent members access to a long pool surrounded by chairs and umbrellas, an outdoor café, changing rooms, and a private sandy beach on the Atlantic Ocean. Arriving, Jon slips into the water beside Dave at the lower end of the pool. Instead of waiting for Jon to make his pitch, Dave seizes the initiative.

"So, kid, are you ready to start doing some of my legal work?" Jon is surprised by Dave's directness, but of course elated. Jon gulps. "Sure," he says.

Without another word, Dave pulls himself out of the pool. He heads to the pay phone near the club entrance and calls his project manager.

"Ken, have we given out all of the legal work for the New York Avenue apartment project?" he asks.

"Well, the law firm we currently use has been handling all the work on this," Ken says.

"What about the closing for New York Avenue?"

"No," Ken says, "we haven't yet told them that they'll be doing that."

"Okay, what's the fee for that work?"

"We pay $17,000 for a closing."

Dave hangs up, returns to the pool and lowers himself back into the water.

"Okay, Jon, I want you to do the closing on our New York Avenue apartment project in Atlantic City." He grins. "I'll pay you $17,000."

Jon is in shock; he can't catch his breath and for a second wonders whether he's having a heart attack. The fee that Dave mentions so casually amounts to more than the salary he collects annually as a Legal Aid lawyer. As a new solo practitioner in a fledging law practice, he charges his clients $35 per hour. Then a wave of nerves washes over him. He's never done legal work for a real estate deal and has no idea what's involved. And here is Dave, tossing him into the deep end. Still, Jon quickly recovers and accepts the work. That moment marks the start of Jon's long lawyer relationship with Dave – in some ways a father figure he has known since he was three years old.

As the summer of 1979 draws to an end, Resorts is coming under considerable political pressure to begin investing in and developing housing in Atlantic City. Earlier that year Dave and Pierre Hollingsworth successfully lobbied Perskie to push an amendment to the Casino Control Act to require each casino to make investments in or financing available for housing in Atlantic City. Resorts has already publicly stated, on several occasions that it will develop an urban renewal plan, including hotels, housing and other facilities. James Crosby, the founder and chairman of Resorts, and Jack Davis, the president, are working alongside other senior managers to figure out the details. Both men have heard a lot about Dave's potential housing projects, and the Atlantic City staff keep the duo informed of his gambling. They decide to approach Dave to see if he has any projects coming up in which Resorts could invest. Perhaps more importantly, they want Dave to help Resorts get credit for one or more of his housing projects in Atlantic City.

Davis calls Dave in the Sinatra suite to tell him that Resorts is interested in talking with him about investing in affordable housing. Davis invites him and Louise as the casino's guests to attend the Miss America pageant on September 9 at the Atlantic City Convention Center.

Dave agrees, and calls Louise to tell her. She's ecstatic. She has always wanted to attend the pageant, which in her eyes is one of the most glamorous and exciting events in the country. As the leading business in the city, Resorts is reserving a full row of seats right at the end of the famed runway, affording its guests the best views in the house.

Louise arrives from Elizabeth dressed, as always, in stylish, classic clothes. Before they head off to the pageant, she joins Dave for an early dinner at one of the casino restaurants. After they order, Ben, the sommelier, comes over with the wine. He greets Dave, then asks, innocently, "Where is Mrs. Z tonight?"

Louise looks up at Ben, aghast.

"I'm Mrs. Zarin," she says sternly. Ben is flustered. "Oh, so sorry," he says as he scuttles away.

Louise is indignant.

"How impertinent!. How can he not know who I am? How can he be so stupid?"

What she doesn't acknowledge to herself, and what Dave certainly doesn't volunteer, is that they both know exactly why the hapless Ben is confused. Dave picks up his steak knife and cuts into his very, very rare rib eye, avoiding Louise's glare.

After dinner, Dave and Louise walk over to the convention center where ushers show them to their seats. Crosby motions to Dave, signaling that he should take the empty seat between him and Davis, then introduces Dave to two Resorts managers, Sy Alter and Bob Peloquin. The men take up seats on either side of the trio, leaving Louise to sit between Crosby's girlfriend and Davis' wife.

Alter, a gruff man in his 50s, is Resorts' director of retail sales, real estate projects and special projects in Atlantic City. (Only months later, the Division of Gaming Enforcement will suspend Alter's license over accusations of bribery and procurement of prostitutes.) Bob Peloquin, tall, thin, and athletic looking, is a former prosecutor, who now is president of International Intelligence, Inc., a Resorts subsidiary handling intelligence and security matters.

As the pageant contestants parade along the runway, Crosby and Davis pepper Dave with questions about what projects he already is developing as well as his future plans. The three awkwardly huddle together to hear each other over the cheers of the audience.

Crosby then tells Dave, "As you know, Resorts is committed to investing in and developing housing in Atlantic City."

Dave tells the execs that he's seen the press reports and talked with the local politicos.

"A lot of people are looking to Resorts to lead the way on this. There's a lot of need for housing here, especially for affordable housing. What can I do to help?"

Crosby and Davis look at each other.

"Resorts would be interested in investing in one or more of your projects," Crosby tells Dave. "Perhaps the New York Avenue project? Or, if not that venture, then maybe other projects under development?"

Crosby adds that the income Resorts would generate from the investment isn't the company's primary motivation.

"Rather, Resorts wants to get maximum credit and publicity for our participation. We'd pay a premium; this should be good for you as well."

Dave is silent for a while, then turns to Crosby.

"If you and Jack and other Resorts executives want to make an investment, as private individuals, I'm happy to work with you," Dave says. "The tax shelters would be a good investment for each of you. Individually. We can easily arrive at a fair price."

Dave pauses a moment as the audience breaks into wild applause. Once it quiets down, Dave looks directly at Crosby. "But I won't sell any part of these projects to Resorts. There's such a great need in Atlantic City, Resorts can't use my projects as a way to get around your commitment for housing. I'm sorry."

Dave feels strongly that the casinos need to develop their own affordable housing projects. The housing shortage is too acute for them to merely piggyback on projects already in the works.

Crosby is taken aback; he glares at Dave but holds his anger in check. The men settle back in their seats to watch the rest of the pageant in silence. Pageant M.C. Bert Parks crowns Miss Virginia as the new Miss America and the evening ends. When saying their goodbyes, Crosby asks Dave to continue talking with Sy Alter and Bob Peloquin to see what they can work out.

Dave does meet with Alter and Peloquin; they speak on the phone several times over the next two weeks. But Dave doesn't budge; he insists he'll only sell shares in his projects to the executives on an individual basis, and won't allocate a stake to Resorts. Nevertheless, Alter prepares a press release announcing that Resorts will participate in Dave's projects and sends it to him to review.

"I didn't agree to any of this!" Dave protests angrily. "You can't release this; it's all untrue."

Resorts publicly releases the announcement anyway.

Dave is furious. He issues his own emphatic press release denying that he has reached any kind of deal on housing between his company and Resorts.

∗∗∗

Every day, Gary Grant usually chats with VP James Carr to discuss the gambling activity of the patrons with credit lines who played the night before. Dave, as the casino's biggest customer, is a frequent topic of discussion. How long did he play? How much did he win? It's Carr's job to then update Jack Davis every day on Dave's playing.

In September 1979, Dave begins to spend even more time at the craps table. He frequently starts playing before dinner, breaks to grab a meal, and then returns to the craps table where he stays until late into the night. His overwhelming drive to gamble seems to be distracting him from his stated mission to build affordable housing. He's lost interest in getting daily updates on the progress of his projects, something that further alarms Rich and confuses Dave's longtime staff.

Meanwhile, Martha is playing her own game, aiming to score as many perks as possible from the casinos. She constantly urges Dave to gamble at Caesars and then plays Resorts and Caesars off against one another in pursuit of ever-greater goodies.

On September 29, Dave and Martha head to the craps table in the early evening before dinner. Dave's credit limit is $175,000 that night. His credit balance is $165,000, so he only has $10,000 in credit to play with. Dave starts off by signing a marker for $5,000, and, when a new shooter begins, he increases the amount of his bet.

Over the next two hours, he wins over $15,000. He asks Martha to cash in the chips at the cage so they can go to dinner. He makes one last bet and then walks over to the cage to meet Martha. From a distance, Dave sees her accept an envelope of cash from the cashier – and then watches as she slides several stacks of wrapped $100 bills from the envelope into her purse. Folding the envelope shut, Martha then turns and heads back to the craps table, unaware that Dave is a short distance behind her. When they meet, she casually hands him the envelope with the remaining money. Dave decides to avoid confronting her and acts as if he hadn't noticed.

After dinner, he and Martha return to the craps table, where Dave signs another $5,000 marker. This time Dave is the shooter. He places two $500 chips on the Pass line and throws a 7, instantly doubling his money. He adds the $1,000 winnings to the Pass line. Tonight, Dave's luck continues. He loosens his tie and presses each time his number hits, until each number holds the table limit of $2000.

Dave is having one of those dream winning streaks; the kind that becomes the talk of casinos for months to come. The players at the table yell each time Dave rolls the dice. Dave yells even louder, pumping his fist in the air. He continues to roll the dice without sevening-out for more than 25 minutes.

When he finishes, he has a long line of $500 chips stacked in front of him, totaling $45,000. For once, Dave's luck holds for the rest of the night. Each shooter at the table has unusually long rolls of the dice before rolling a seven. Every time the dice return to Dave, players and spectators crowd around the table. By now Dave's face is aglow with a sheen of perspiration. He's in the zone, Martha can tell from the look on his face. Everyone, even casino employees, are caught up in the electrifying excitement. Dave keeps playing until around 2 a.m., winning over $110,000.

When he quits playing, Dave covers his chips with his hands as Martha moves to pick them up.

"That's okay, Martha, I'll take them over to the cashier's cage myself," he tells her.

He hands over $80,000 in chips at the cashier's cage in exchange for an equivalent amount in markers. He then swaps the rest of the chips for cash and immediately stores the money in the hotel's safe deposit box. The next morning Dave deposits the cash at his bank so that checks he has written to Resorts will clear.

By now almost every time Dave comes to play, crowds form around the craps table to watch his gambling high-wire act. He sparks an excitement and energy no other player can match. Resorts is abuzz whenever its star customer is on the floor. Resorts officials congratulate themselves for keeping their prized gambler from defecting to one of the new Atlantic City rivals. And they are working hard to keep him happy.

But regulators decide that the casino is trying too hard.

On October 3, 1979, the Division of Gaming Enforcement files a complaint against Resorts with the Casino Control Commission, alleging 809 violations of the casino regulations pertaining to its credit procedures as well as its internal administrative and accounting controls. About 100 of these violations involve the way the casino extends credit to Dave and Martha.

The complaint names people who deal extensively with Dave: Irv Rogers, James Carr, Gary Thompson and Gary Grant. The regulators ask the commission to order Resorts to cease issuing credit to any customer whose credit reference card exceeds the approved credit limit (a direct challenge to the TTO system) and to require the credit manager to include as credit all uncleared personal checks patrons give them to pay off a marker. If the Casino Control Commission acts on these measures, it will wreak havoc on Dave's ability to keep playing. But when, on October 9, one of the commissioners issues an emergency order, it only requires the casino to include as credit all "undeposited checks" received in payment of a marker.

Resorts easily gets around this minor irritant. The casino simply uses a TTO to boost Dave's credit limit until the check is deposited by the casino the next morning.

This tactic allows Dave to gamble just as aggressively as ever, with the casino's cooperation. Dave's case highlights lax oversight.

Even after the casino runs a routine credit check of Dave's two New Jersey bank accounts, which show a balance of $50,000 in one account, and in the other a mere $300, it doesn't blink.

If Resorts doesn't seem worried by Dave's increasingly frenetic gambling, Sol Henkind's anxiety level is soaring. Sol is now Dave's business partner in the Atlantic City Apartments, the 175-unit high-rise building, and for the Liberty project, the rehabilitation of the Liberty Hotel, the YMCA and the schoolhouse. The men have collaborated reasonably well over the years, but one night Sol has a dream about Dave playing craps – and Sol then falls out of bed. Spooked by the incident, Sol wants out; he can't stomach Dave's risk-taking any longer.

Dave now has to find another partner group to take over Sol's interest. But Dave has to repay Sol his initial $290,000 investment to close the transaction. Feeling stuck and anxious, Dave discusses the topic with Martha over dinner, talking through his options as she listens silently. The next morning, without saying anything, Martha arranges a wire transfer of $290,000 to Dave's bank account.

Dave is shocked, elated, and grateful. He can't get over Martha's gesture. He asks her why she sent the money.

"You needed it, so I sent it to you," Martha says, matter-of-factly.

"I'll get it back to you as soon as I can," Dave says, relieved. "I promise."

Later that month, the National Bank in Elizabeth calls Dave about checks coming through the bank for clearance and payment to Resorts Casino on almost a daily basis. The bank has made several loans to Dave and his companies and now it has questions about his gambling habit. Dave, irritated by the bank's questions, complains to Martha.

"Well, to get them off your back, why don't I pay off your markers using one of my personal checks," she suggests. "Then you can pay me back with your own check. I'll deposit your check into my bank in Montreal."

They soon form a routine: If Martha is in the casino with Dave, she writes the checks to Resorts. Dave then repays Martha at the end of every evening. If Martha isn't at the casino, Dave writes a personal check to Resorts. In November, Dave signs a third promissory note to Martha for $200,000. A fourth note follows in December, this one for $90,000. Dave has now promised to pay Martha nearly $500,000.

***

In late November, Dave and his team prepare to close on the financing that will allow them to begin construction of the 175-unit senior citizen housing project at New York Avenue. The interest rate they'll pay for the money, provided by the New Jersey Housing Finance Agency, is well below market rate. Kevin Quinn, a tall Black junior development officer leads the HFA team closing on behalf of the agency. Jon Epstein, now handling the legal work for Dave on his first project, arranges to meet with Kevin before the closing. Since becoming Dave's attorney, Jon has been working to learn the ins and outs of commercial real estate law. Jon is personable and outgoing; Kevin is more reserved. They exchange pleasantries, then Jon puts his cards on the table.

"Look, we've never met before, but I'm the straightest guy you will ever know, and I'm going to tell you something." Jon pauses. "I don't know what the fuck I'm doing."

Kevin's mouth drops as he stares at Jon, who is smiling a bit sheepishly back at him. Kevin likes Jon's directness and returns the grin.

"Don't worry Jon. We'll get the deal closed."

It's the beginning of a close working relationship between them. (Kevin would later become executive director of the agency.)

***

My sister Robin, living in Chicago with her boyfriend Larry, announces their engagement. At the age of 25, Robin now has a master's degree in deaf education and is teaching at a school for the hearing impaired in Chicago. Larry is head of admissions at a technical college in Chicago. To celebrate, Resorts hosts an engagement party for the couple and their families on Thanksgiving weekend. Robin and Larry, Larry's mom and stepfather, Rich and his wife Susan, Dave and Louise–and of course Martha–are guests at a private dinner at Le Relais, the elegant French restaurant at Resorts.

Robin designs the seating arrangement, placing Dave and Louise next to each other and Martha, the one non-family member, at the other end of the table. Robin doesn't know Martha well, nor does she understand her relationship with her father. While Robin has spoken to her briefly a few times, she believes that she's merely a family friend and Dave's business associate.

The elegant dinner puts all the guests in a festive mood. Everyone, that is, except for Martha, who seethes in silence over her foie gras. After dinner, Martha takes Dave aside to complain.

"Robin is trying to separate us," she says in barely controlled anger. "You can't let her insult me like that."

As the party guests head back to their rooms, Dave asks to talk with Robin privately. They go up to the Sinatra suite; in the master bedroom Dave turns to Robin.

"Why did you seat Martha so far away from me at the table?" he asks accusingly. "What was your aim in separating us?"

His voice is rising in anger. "Why would you snub Martha like that?"

Robin is shocked.

"What are you talking about?" she asks.

"Martha says you're trying to separate us," he barks.

Robin's mouth drops. It's starting to dawn on her that Dave and Martha are anything but platonic business associates. Robin blanches.

"I don't even know what you are talking about!" She rushes out of the room, slamming the door behind her.

Once Dave is back downstairs at the craps table, Robin returns to the Sinatra suite to talk with Louise about Martha – but stops short of saying she thinks the two are having an affair.

"Mom, it's obvious that she is controlling Dad. You shouldn't stand for this."

Louise is stunned by Robin's insinuation. She has convinced herself that Martha is merely a close business associate and nothing more. It is not unusual for Dave to have women friends and business associates.

"Mom I think you should leave Dad," Robin says flatly.

Louise gasps, and her eyes widen.

"But where am I going to go? This is a couples world. What would I do without him? I've spent most of my life with him," she says.

Louise sits on the sofa, her shoulders hunched in despair. Robin's confrontation forced Louise to part the blinders she had been hiding behind for so long. She couldn't and wouldn't even consider what Dave was up to with that woman. It was strictly business; it had to be, she thought. No, Robin had it wrong. Women were always attracted to Dave. That was true throughout their marriage – even before, during high school and beyond. And, what if it were true – what could she do? No, she's loved him since she was 13. No matter what he did – and he's done a lot, she would always love him. Divorce is not an option; an unacceptable embarrassment. Middle class Jewish women did not get divorced. Plus, in all honesty, if she couldn't rely on Dave taking care of her financially, how would she support herself? What about the family? No, Robin is wrong. Period.

Louise turns back to Robin. "Martha may control him, but your dad is not sleeping with her," Louise insists. "I know he wouldn't. She is not very attractive and she is so pushy and full of herself. He'd never be attracted to a woman like that."

Robin's eyebrows shoot up in surprise at Louise's naïve comment. Realizing that Dave's infidelity is too painful and too scary for Louise to acknowledge, Robin drops the subject.

Frustrated by Louise's denial and sense of helplessness, Robin becomes even more upset with her father. The next day, Robin stops Dave near the hotel entrance. In a low voice she tells Dave she had a conversation with Louise, but doesn't offer any details. It's plain to Dave that Robin is fuming.

"I've had time to think this over," she says. "And I don't ever want to see you again." Then she walks out of the hotel.

In shock, Dave watches the hotel's doors slide shut behind her back. He immediately returns to the suite to ask Louise what Robin told her. He finds Louise packing her bag and getting ready to leave, a day earlier than planned.

"I just know that you really upset her, Dave," Louise says, ducking the main question but still challenging her husband.

"It's a special weekend for her and she's your only daughter. You should make up with her."

Louise snaps shut her suitcase just as the bellman calls to tell her the limo is ready. Without so much as a glance at Dave, Louise marches out of the suite and rides the comped casino limo back to their apartment in Elizabeth.

Dave is upset by the family turmoil and blames Martha for instigating the fights. He knocks on Martha's door. When she opens, he stands stiffly in the hallway.

"Pack up your things and get out of my life. Leave me – and my family – alone."

Having delivered his ultimatum, Dave turns and strides away, leaving Martha wide-eyed and with her mouth agape.

He heads outside to the boardwalk to cool down. He isn't wearing a coat or gloves, but doesn't seem to notice the icy ocean wind whipping his hair and tie. Nor does he notice a woman clad in a voluminous lynx coat and a matching fur hat following him. Martha gradually catches up to Dave and places a gloved hand on his arm.

"Please Dave, I'm sorry you're so upset. You know I'd never do anything to hurt you. Please, let's talk this over."

Dave roughly shakes off her hand and glares at her.

"My family is the most important thing to me, Martha. I want you out of my life."

At that, Martha stops short and grips Dave's arm. "Oh no you don't," she says, through gritted teeth.

"You're not getting off the hook that easily. I'll get out of your life only when I'm good and ready to go."

Suddenly, Martha's face softens; she lapses into a plea.

"Dave, we have such a good thing, let's keep it that way. And besides, who's going to keep you company at the tables?"

She gives him a playful, yet saccharine smile.

"We need to keep you winning so that you can pay me back."

At that Dave slows to a stop, deflated; his shoulders rounding. Martha loops her arm through Dave's and gently, firmly steers him back to the hotel.

When it comes to Dave's loyalty, Louise clearly won this battle, Martha thinks irritably.

"But I'm going to win the war," she tells herself. "It'll just take more time."

Some weeks later, Dave asks Robin and Louise to meet him at a local hamburger restaurant in Elizabeth.

When they settle into a booth, Dave says, "I am sorry about our fight. There is nothing more important to me than my family. I don't want to lose you guys."

Beseeching their forgiveness, he continues, "I don't want you to be angry with me. We need to get past this."

After a short period of silence, Louise puts out her hands, placing one on Dave's and the other on Robin's.

"I want things back to normal, too, Dave. Family first. That's how it should be." Louise looks at Robin expectantly.

But Robin is tougher to win over. It takes several minutes before she concedes, answering, "Okay, Mom." She turns to Dave, but without a smile.

"I'm doing this for Mom, and for the good of the family. But I hope this is the last of this – um – misunderstanding."

Dave hangs his head, ashamed, relieved and grateful to Robin for not dredging up the cause of the fight.

Family first.

Somehow, they manage to put the dispute behind them without ever mentioning Martha.

CHAPTER 7: THE PRICE OF EUPHORIA

On December 22,1979, Atlantic City's *The Press* publishes an article highlighting the way that Dave's companies are dramatically improving the city's housing shortage. The article reports that Dave spent $79 million to build new affordable housing in 1979 and expects to spend nearly triple that sum in 1980, or about $200 million.

"We are planning to begin building 1500 middle income homes in the county," Dave tells the reporter.

"This figure", he adds, "includes 800 market rental units and 200 more subsidized units."

The positive media coverage underscores Dave's growing stature outside the casino as David Zarin, the business mover and shaker with the financial and political clout to make his affordable housing projects a reality.

"Welcome, Mr. Zarin," is a familiar greeting; one Dave hears from owners and staff whenever he visits his favorite steakhouse or oyster bar. They like Mr. Zarin, and he's a good tipper, so they make sure he gets the VIP treatment.

At the same time, the casino's Mr. Z also enjoys a degree of celebrity – not as a shrewd businessman, but as a profitable customer; one of Resorts' biggest spenders. Dave increasingly seems to have two identities: one as Mr. David Zarin and the other as Mr. Z.

Martha, meanwhile, is luxuriating in the pampering and freebies offered to Mr. Z and his guests. She prods Dave to play more at Caesar's casino, so that she can enjoy their generous comps as well as those offered by Resorts. Caesars gives Dave and Martha each a credit limit of $200,000. Then, as a holiday gift, the casino sends them state-of-the-art large screen televisions in polished pecan wood cabinets. One goes to Dave's home in Elizabeth; another to Martha's place in Montreal. The casino sweetens the pot further when it offers Dave and Martha the use of its private 60-foot yacht for a weekend in the Bahamas; it even flies them to Miami, where the yacht is moored.

For Martha, every comp, large or small, is a personal win, and she's keeping score. Decked out in a low-cut turquoise sundress and a wide-brimmed straw hat, she boards the yacht with Dave, and peers over her Chanel sunglasses as she marvels at its luxurious appointments. It has an upper and lower deck, as well as a beautiful outdoor sitting area. The indoor couches and seats are in leather; each of the two large staterooms features a king-size bed. That first night, Martha snuggles against Dave on the couch as she sips a glass of wine.

"You may get your kicks from gambling, but for me, this is what it is all about." she purrs. Ironically, they spend the weekend gambling not at Caesars, but at the Resorts casino on Paradise Island. Thanks to Gary Grant's diligence, they receive the same pampering they enjoy in Atlantic City.

But the growing competition with Caesars for Mr. Z's patronage at the tables is beginning to alarm Crosby and Davis at Resorts. Another potential rival, Bally's Park

Place Casino, is opening soon and they know that more casinos will follow suit in the coming two years. Now, they ask themselves: Just how valuable is Mr. Z to our Atlantic City operation?

They dig through their records, pull out their Red Book, and total Dave's losses since June 1978. As of October 1979, Dave has lost (and paid to Resorts) about $2.5 million (the equivalent of over $11.8 million in 2024). An excellent Resorts customer, indeed!

The casino's managers have long understood that one of the best ways to keep Dave's business is through his "lady friend" Martha. Davis calls a meeting with his top lieutenants, including Jim Carr, to discuss Mr. Z and Martha. "For the time being we'll send Dave and Martha Piaget diamond and gold watches," Davis informs his team. "They're about $5,000 each. But I want all of you to think about what else can we do for them."

Carr is the first to offer a suggestion. "Zarin is constantly complain-ing about his credit limit at the casino and constantly pressing Gary to increase his limits," he says. "Perhaps we should do something along those lines."

"What if we remove any credit limit, and let him gamble for as long and as much as he wants? Would that satisfy Zarin?" Davis asks.

"It sure would," Carr says. "But how do we do that without running afoul of the casino regulations?"

This is a real concern, but the casino executives come up with a way around it. Davis suggests that the casino clear all of Zarin's checks immediately and that Grant and the credit folks TTO him for an unlimited amount and for an unlimited period.

"You know," Davis muses aloud, "if he loses enough money, he may be more receptive to a Resorts investment in his housing—."

Davis catches himself, and abruptly turns to Carr, "Okay, remove his credit limit. Make it happen."

When Dave returns to Resorts in the New Year, Grant tells him he doesn't have to worry about bumping up against credit limits anymore.

"You won't have a credit limit from now on," Grant tells him.

Resorts will consider all of his checks cleared as soon as he's written them and will give him unlimited TTOs, Grant adds, for an unlimited period, for as long as Dave wants. Dave doesn't grasp the procedural details Grant describes. All he hears is: "You have unlimited credit."

Dave's face lights up. Up to now, those credit limits have always curbed Dave's gambling. When he played poker or went to the racetrack, he gambled only with the money he brought with him. Credit limits at the casinos in Las Vegas or the Bahamas served as guardrails that kept him from crashing and burning. Now, Resorts has torn out the last guardrail.

Dave is jubilant.

"Finally, I'll be able to win!"

That night he's too excited to sleep, like a kid on Christmas Eve. His heart races; he imagines himself shooting the dice, pressing every bet, and winning every roll. Despite a fitful night's sleep, the next morning he feels buoyant and optimistic. He orders a big breakfast, so he won't have to stop gambling for lunch. His mind is already on the action at the craps table as he finishes his coffee. He hurries down to the casino and barely registers the time: 10:30 a.m. Having his credit limit removed is the boost Dave has been counting on. And now he's stepping on the gas.

The casino's personnel are surprised and pleased to see Dave on the floor so early in the day. They notice there's something different about him. Everyone on the floor feels it. And they also know the energy levels within the casino will rev up once Dave starts gambling.

This early in the day, there are only three other players at Dave's preferred table. Dave greets the dealers, and a couple of the players by name. He feels exhilarated as he arranges his chips on the rail in front of him; he self-consciously lowers his hands below the table's edge and rubs them together with excitement. He takes a deep breath, rests his hands lightly on the rail again, and straightens his back. The adrenaline rush has begun. Time to play. Dave places $2,000 in chips on the table's Pass line, with a dramatic snap. He turns his eyes to the shooter and holds his breath.

The dice roller hits the number "9". Dave follows up, placing a $4,000 bet behind the Pass line and another $1,000 in chips on each of the point numbers 4, 5, 6, 8, and 10. He has a total of $11,000 on the table. Dave wins his bet on a specific number if he rolls the number "9" or a point number. He loses all of his bets on the table if he rolls the number "7". When point numbers hit, Dave presses his bet, up to the maximum allowable bet of $2,000 per number. When the dice roller sevens-out after only a few rolls, Dave loses all of the money on the table. He signs another marker for $10,000. He continues to play in the same manner, always daring, always pressing.

Fresh from her complimentary massage and facial, Martha joins Dave in the middle of the afternoon He hasn't taken a break since he started playing that morning. He's lost more than he's won. Yet he keeps chasing his losses, convinced he'll soon hit big. Martha begins signing markers and gets a TTO for an additional $50,000. As usual, the dealer passes Martha's chips to Dave to play. Dave and Martha continue playing craps until 1:30 in the next morning, stopping only to grab a quick dinner. By the time he finally quits for the night, he has said goodnight to two shifts of dealers; the third table team of the evening is amazed by both Dave's stamina and his bullet-proof confidence he'll hit big on the next roll.

Even as the casino staff recognize that a "new" Dave has showed up at the craps table, Rich is worried about changes in Dave's attention span. Dave does manage to pull himself away from Atlantic City for staff meetings in Elizabeth or Harrisburg, but he's irritable and distracted. The Dave Zarin they knew was always demanding status updates from each employee and asking pointed follow-up questions. This new Dave feels like a stranger. Instead of delving into the weeds on every project, Dave – now Mr. Z – seems less interested in project details. Even when it comes to reviewing and approving project budgets, Rich can't get Dave to focus.

Back in Elizabeth, Louise is beginning to understand and empathize with friends who moan about being "golf widows." The fact that Dave is away from home managing his volatile business, rather than chasing a little ball across the greens, brings her little comfort.

On the other hand, Louise enjoys her independence. Between weekly bridge and Mahjong games with friends, and volunteering twice a week working with infants at a pediatric renal clinic, she is busy and feels fulfilled. But Dave's long absences are fueling a low-simmering resentment of his passion for gambling – gambling that is increasingly worrying her .

On the few occasions she's recently visited Dave at the casino, she can see the hold that craps seems to have on him. How it seems to crowd out everything else: his family, his friends and maybe even his business. She's always kept quiet about her concerns, but now decides she needs to speak up. She pushes away from her unfinished dinner and picks up the phone to talk with Rich. Maybe she's worrying for nothing; Rich will tell her.

"Don't worry, Mom," Rich says, reassuringly. "You know how focused Dad gets about his projects, especially now that they are in development. But I'll talk to him and tell him you miss him."

Wanting to spare Louise any further anxiety, Rich avoids sharing his own concerns about Dave's gambling. But the next time Rich gets Dave alone, he asks him, point-blank, what is going on.

"Dad, you're not yourself, you spend most of your time at the casino in Atlantic City, it's sometimes hard to get you on the phone," he says, gently.

"Mom's worried about you. She misses you. And I'm worried about you – and the business."

Rich knows Dave may get angry, but he forges ahead anyway.

"Is it the gambling that's distracting you?"

Dave's face hardens. "Don't tell me how to run the business," he snaps at Rich. "There is a lot going on in

Atlantic City and I need to devote a lot of my time to moving these projects along and meeting with people. The pressure is intense."

Dave then falls back on his customary self-justification.

"I need to relax. I know what I am doing, and don't question me," he says in a gravelly voice. "So I take little breaks from time to time. So what?"

The problem is that Dave's "little breaks" aren't so little. Dave begins to spend 15 or 16 hours a day at the tables – day after day after day. What Dave doesn't realize, and what he certainly couldn't find the right words to explain to Rich, is that the business is no longer his passion – his mistress, gambling, has taken over control. He's tired of juggling so many deals. Overseeing details, evaluating financial risks, enduring the agonizingly slow process of getting approvals, and the difficulties of financing and selling projects: It's grinding.

But playing craps! What an adrenaline rush! Fewer complications; you win, or you lose, and you move on to the next toss of the dice. Each roll is a new fix for Dave's inner adrenaline junkie. His problems and worries evaporate. When he picks up the dice, all is forgotten. And, he tells himself, that if he wins on the toss, all is forgiven, too.

Until the next roll, that is. Dave rarely touches the free martinis that appear on his drink rail. He doesn't need the alcohol to give him a buzz. The game itself delivers an intoxicating cocktail of anxiety, euphoria, regret, and hope whose effects last well into the night. In that fugue state, Dave loses track of time as well as the number of markers he is signing. The circles under his eyes are deeper and darker than ever. Night after night, a well-rested, well-fed and well-coiffed Martha stands beside him, encouraging him to keep playing and handing over her chips. When he's too exhausted to see the table clearly, he stumbles off toward the elevator, with Martha guiding him. When he tumbles into bed, all that is on his mind is starting again early the next morning.

By now, Dave and Martha are writing personal checks for more than $20,000 every day. In mid-January, Dave's "official" credit line, as detailed on his credit reference card remains $200,000, but Grant and the casino execs have signed off on a TTO of $503,000. Martha's actual credit line is $100,000; on January 16, she has a TTO totaling $603,000. Fearful that Resorts might cut off the unlimited credit spigot, Dave and Martha continue writing personal checks to pay the markers. To cover these checks, Dave begins cashing non-gaming personal checks at the casino cage in outsize amounts: $10,000, $25,000 and $60,000. He puts the stacks of $100 bills, bundled in Resorts bill wrappers, into brown bags, then places them in his safe deposit box at Resorts. The next morning, he puts the bags of cash into his briefcase, walks several blocks from the casino to the local Guarantee Bank, and deposits the money into his account. When Dave wins at the craps table, he cashes in the chips instead of redeeming markers, and then deposits the money in his local bank account to cover the checks he wrote to Resorts the previous week.

With such high stakes, the casino designates a security guard to stand several feet behind Dave at the craps table to make sure that no one steals his chips while he is playing. The guard then escorts Dave from the casino to his safe deposit box in the hotel. But no guards accompany him on his daily trips to the bank to deposit the cash.

Dave is so caught up in the constant shuffle of checks, cash and markers, that he no longer keeps track of it all. He is on a merry-go-round that is spinning ever faster: He uses casino money to cover the checks he and Martha write to the casino so he can keep gambling. When Martha is in town, she writes most of the personal checks to Resorts and then collects a personal check from Dave each night to cover the total amount.

The first signs that real financial trouble is brewing come at the end of January, when Dave's bank returns several of the checks he has written to Martha for insufficient funds. Dave asks Martha to hold onto his checks; he can't immediately deposit enough cash to cover all of them.

"I need you to do this for me. You know I'm good for it," he says.

Martha hesitates. Seeing his handsome face, her reluctance melts away.

"All right, Dave." she replies. "I trust you."

She puts the uncashed checks in an envelope in her hotel room drawer. Dave also asks Martha to give him blank checks made out to Resorts so he can fill in the totals and use them to gamble when she is not there. She agrees.

A few events do seem to interrupt Dave's gambling fever. One of these is a luncheon at Bally's Casino. On Saturday, January 26, 1980, the Atlantic City Chamber of Commerce honors Dave, with the title of the "Most

Progressive Businessman Award". Many of the city's leading politicians, businessmen, and community leaders are there to applaud and acknowledge the significant progress Dave is making in increasing the availability of affordable housing in Atlantic City.

Dave, in a dark blue suit and red tie, and Louise, elegantly dressed in a stylish ecru skirt, jacket, and cream silk blouse are a striking couple. Across the table from them, Rich regards them with pride. Even at the ages of 62, his parents still turn heads. His mother, the picture of class, couldn't be a greater contrast to Martha, seated beside Rich and his wife, Susan. Wearing a navy blue shift, big diamond rings and Mobe pearl earrings the size of silver dollars, Martha oozes an aura of showy self-importance that grates on Rich. He turns his head away from her. This is Dave's celebration, and Louise's, and Rich doesn't want anything to distract him from enjoying their moment.

After a glowing introduction from the mayor, Dave goes to the podium to receive his award, pausing to inspect the brass and wood plaque.

"The world is watching us," Dave tells the crowd in his accept-ance speech. "Will development in Atlantic City be limited to the boardwalk and marina, the mere movie set where casinos operate and tourists flock?"

Dave looks over the crowd for a moment.

"Or, will the benefits of casino gambling extend beyond this, to the people who build, live and work in this city?"

The crowd is riveted as Dave continues.

"We must ensure that everyone in this community fully participates in this resurgence. The heart of this revival is housing, and in particular affordable housing."

Dave holds up the plaque and nods.

"Thank you for this honor."

The audience erupts into applause, and gives him a standing ovation. Martha beams at Dave, with possessive pride. As Dave returns to his chair, he pats Rich on the back, and gently squeezes Louise's shoulder in a surprising gesture of tenderness. Martha flinches, but keeps a smile on her face. Rich can't recall the last time he saw his father show Louise affection, or that he'd seen Louise so happy, so proud.

When lunch is over, however, Dave transforms, once again, into Mr. Z, and heads back to the craps table. Louise returns to the empty apartment in Elizabeth, and Martha resumes her role as Dave's gambling companion.

***

Throughout the early weeks of 1980, Jack Davis keeps urging Steve Norton, the executive vice president of Resorts, to reach out again to Dave to discuss the possibility of Resorts investing in his housing projects. Steve meets Dave for lunch and has several telephone discussions with him during January and February. But the freshly anointed "most progressive businessman" of Atlantic City continues to rebuff Resorts' request.

He may turn down Resorts' money for his projects, but Dave is still delighted to tap into the casino's unlimited credit line to gamble. On Friday, January 29, Dave is back at the craps table early again. Always wanting to ratchet up the excitement, he asks the boxman to increase the maximum bet on each point number from $2,000 to $2,500. The boxman turns to the pit boss standing behind him and gets a nod. "Okay," says the boxman. The chutzpah! Other players around the table exchange glances and stare at Dave with admiration, but say nothing.

When a new roller begins, Dave places $2,500 in chips on the Pass line. A "6" is rolled. Dave places $7,500 behind the Pass line, and places $2,500 in chips on each of the numbers 4, 5, 8, 9 and 10. Dave now is risking a total of $22,500 in chips (equivalent to $106,000 in today's dollars) on each roll of the dice. Word of Dave's bold bets and the new, gutsy maximum flies across the casino floor. Ever larger crowds begin gathering around the craps table, with those on the outer ring craning their necks to catch the action. Dave, who once basked in the excitement and attention of the spectators, is too dazed to notice the cheers and applause. There's no room in his mind for anything but the next roll; the next sip of that intoxicant called craps. He must continue to play, to survive, to continue the rush.

Over the three-day weekend, Dave is TTO'ed up to $871,000, even while his credit reference card still reflects a permanent credit line of $200,000. Martha has a TTO of up to $420,000. Her credit reference card shows a permanent credit line of $100,000. The "official" numbers are becoming more illusory by the day. By the end of January, Dave effectively is gambling with a credit line of $1,291,000 (equal to $6.1 million in today's dollars). Over the course of the month, he signs markers totaling $1,385,000 (equivalent to $6.5 million today) and cashes non-gaming personal checks totaling $275,000 (or about $1.3 million today).

On the Sunday night at the end of the three-day weekend, Dave is distraught, depressed, and panicky. In a rare moment of lucidity, Dave realizes that he has no idea how much money he has lost, only that it is a catastrophic amount and a sum that he has no way to repay. He's beside himself with anxiety, which at least for the moment, overtakes his compulsion to gamble. As he walks through the casino, he spots Gary Grant and rushes up to him, visibly agitated.

"I can't for the life of me understand why you give me so much credit!" Dave exclaims. "How the hell can you rationalize this and do this to me – to anyone?" Dave glares at Gary.

"When I started gambling here back in June 1978, I had just paid you back $20,000 I owed Resorts for years." Dave struggles to regain his composure.

"I don't understand why you allow me so much credit!" He pauses to take a deep breath. "I never really asked you for unlimited credit. Never!"

Grant, who in some respects considers Dave a friend, is stung and angered by this sudden about-face. But he shows no emotion.

"Look Dave," he says, neutrally, "I suggest you take time to calm down. Get a good night's rest and let's talk this over in the morning."

Grant reports the incident to Carr, noting that Dave and Martha together have a TTO of well above a million dollars. Although it's after midnight, Carr calls Jack Davis to fill him in. Mr. Z is by far the casino's biggest, most important player, far more valued than the other two dozen or so players awarded Resorts' elite rating. Carr tells Davis how much money Zarin has lost.

"What should we do?" he asks.

Davis doesn't hesitate.

"Let him go. Keep it going. We need to keep him as a customer."

Despite what Dave told Grant in a moment of panic and depression just days earlier, he's more terrified of being cut off from gambling. He borrows $300,000 from one of his West Coast business partners. For collateral, he uses some of his future profits on the New York Avenue Section 8 project that's now under development. He also continues borrowing from his companies. Whenever Dave is short of funds in his personal bank accounts to cover the checks he and Martha are writing to Resorts, he borrows money, cashes non-gaming personal checks at Resorts for deposit in his bank account, or converts the gaming chips into cash for deposit at his bank. He rarely redeems his or Martha's markers. He also begins cashing, as non-gaming checks, some of Martha's blank checks and also deposits that money in his bank account.

Throughout February, Dave leaves the casino with $50,000 to $100,000 in cash daily to deposit at his bank, in a desperate scramble to cover the checks he and Martha are writing to Resorts. On several occasions, Dave has his bank issue a cashier's check to Martha to deposit in her Canadian bank account, so that the checks she writes to Resorts don't bounce. He gives Resorts postdated personal checks totaling $200,000 – and takes back his markers for an equivalent amount.

In mid-February, Martha is putting away her negligée when she spots the envelope containing all Dave's uncashed checks in the dresser drawer. Without thinking, she removes it, takes out the checks, and begins to add up the amounts. They now total $1,680,000. She freaks out. Just as Dave hasn't been monitoring how much he has been losing, she hasn't been tracking how much of her cash has been vanishing into Dave's passion for the craps tables. More than a million dollars? Closing in on *two* million dollars? For the past several months, Martha was only dimly aware of the large sums Dave was gambling, but it hadn't worried her. She knew the moment they met that he was destined for big things, big successes, big money. He'll always come out ahead, she had reasoned.

But this! Millions of dollars! An astonishing sum. For the first time, Martha is afraid. What if Dave isn't invincible – then what will happen to her? And to her son? It's not as if she can count on Dave for financial support – he's not her husband! If anything happens to Dave, she'll be left with no leverage to recoup her money. The housing developments, Dave's savings and life insurance: all will go to Louise.

Martha wheels around and charges through the connecting door to Dave's suite where he's sitting on the couch. Standing over him, she brandishes the checks. "What have you been *doing?* What have you done to me?" she shouts at him. "My accounts are bleeding red ink!" Dave looks up at her.

"Calm down," he orders her, in his "I'm-the-boss" voice. "I'll take care of this. I promise."

Dave calls Jon Epstein. He takes care to keep his tone casual and mask his agitation.

"Martha is lending me some money," he tells Jon. "I want to give her a security interest in my projects. Can you draft the papers and come down here tomorrow morning?"

The next morning Jon arrives at the Sinatra suite where he finds Dave and Martha finishing breakfast. Jon hands Dave the draft papers to review, and turns to Martha.

"You should have your own lawyer review the agreement," Jon tells her.

Martha leans back in her chair and looks at Jon.

"Jonnie, Johnnie, you're like family. You know, if I can't trust you, who can I trust? Why would I need my own lawyer?"

Jon shakes his head.

"Martha, you really should have your own lawyer. I'll tell you what, I'll—"

Martha interrupts him.

"Well, I don't want to pay for a lawyer."

"Martha, I'll pay the lawyer," Dave interjects. Let us get someone for you."

Jon offers to find someone to read over the documents at "friends and family rates," so that she will have independent advice. Martha quickly agrees and Jon calls a friend of his, Mickey Weintraub, who arrives the next evening for a dinner meeting with Dave, Martha and Jon. Over the next several weeks, they hammer out a security agreement, one compli-cated by Martha's numerous changes and conditions. Martha insists on getting the same interest that Rich – Dave's son and business partner – has in the Zarin family partnership. The security documents also give Martha a portion of Dave's share in the net profits of Marina Towers, a property still in the development stage. The final agreement also assigns to her, as collateral, all of

Dave's ownership interest in the Zarin family companies as well as his ownership interest in the management company he owns jointly with Rich.

And there's more: Martha has always resented the fact that Louise is the beneficiary of Dave's $1 million life insurance policy. So she insists on having a policy in her favor, too. Initially she demands a matching $1 million policy. Then she doubles the amount, and insists the policy should be worth $2 million. Exasperated, Dave finally purchases two $1 million dollar policies, with Martha as the beneficiary, after taking a physical exam – one that Martha arranges.

During this period, when Rich and Jon are both in Atlantic City, they frequently lament Dave's gambling problem. One evening, Jon spends 15 to 20 minute intervals watching Dave at the table, and notices significant changes in the way he plays. Dave is now much more intense – almost grim – as he puts down his chips; and the bets seem bigger and bolder, almost reckless. When he sevens-out, Dave is sweating and yanks at his tie and unbuttons the top of his shirt. He appears transfixed, in another world. How on earth, Jon wonders, can he find this *fun?*

Shortly thereafter, Jon calls Rich, worried about Dave's state of mind.

"He's so immersed in the game, it's almost robotic," he tells my brother. "He is under extraordinary stress. Rich, I don't see how he is enjoying this. He doesn't seem to be in control."

Rich calls me immediately to share Jon's concerns. After a year working on the Pacific Island of Palau, I'm back in the U.S. and living and working in Washington, D.C.

"Don, I can't get Dave to focus on all these business crises I see on the horizon –things that only Dave can deal with." Rich tells me. "We're trying to convince Dave to slow down his gambling. But no dice, he won't listen."

"I'll come down to Atlantic City next weekend. Let's meet there and you and I can talk with Dave," I tell Rich.

The next weekend, I drive to Atlantic City to talk to Dave about his gambling. Together, Rich and I corner Dave in his suite at Resorts and plead with him to stop.

Dave gives us the same reply we've grown sick of hearing.

"It's under control, stop worrying."

By now, we don't see him as being in control of his gambling. Rather, it's controlling him. I feel I'm watching a car veering off the highway and heading toward the edge of a cliff.

In fact, Dave is grossly overextended. He's rich by 1980 standards, but not rich enough to gamble and lose at this rate. Although Dave doesn't realize it yet, he's effectively lost all of the money he makes or will ever make from his housing projects. To offset his losses, Dave has sold most of his assets, and waved goodbye to any future revenues from his housing projects still under development. He's borrowed extensively from banks and business associates. And he's deeply in debt to Martha. He still has some projects in the pipeline and in the planning stages, but he won't receive any cash flow from those until they're completed.

This nightmare puts Rich under extraordinary stress. There's little he can do to get Dave to recognize the crisis that the family's business faces. Nor can he convince Dave to consider the future of his family. While Dave and Rich work together reasonably well, Dave has a short fuse and Rich hates confrontation. That makes it still harder for us to force Dave to stop and think about the impact of his gambling on others. We all know trouble is looming. The only real question is when – and how abruptly – the merry-go-round will stop.

During February, Dave plays craps for 17 days in a row, often for more than 15 hours each day. He signs an additional $2 million (equivalent to $9.5 million today) in markers, and cashes additional non-gaming personal checks of $585,000 ($2.7 million in today's terms). Dave by now is beginning to feel trapped and powerless. Gambling leaves him feeling exhausted and sick to his stomach. But he still is so enthralled by the highs and lows of the game, he doesn't see how his compulsion is affecting his health.

In early March, Louise comes down to Atlantic City to join Dave at dinner with Dave's brother Ira, and Ira's wife, Ellen, at one of the restaurants in Resorts. When Ira and Ellen spot Dave approaching them, they're alarmed: Though he is as dapper as ever, Dave seems haggard and stressed. Ira wonders how long it's been since his brother had a decent night's sleep. Adding to their concern and confusion, Dave is accompanied not only by Louise, but also by his 'business associate', Martha. Ira and Ellen turn to look at Louise, who greets them warmly, as if nothing is out of the ordinary. Ira shrugs slightly, signaling to Ellen to say nothing. When the maître 'd tells the group their table will be ready in about 15 minutes, Dave gets jumpy.

"I'm going to head off to the craps table and see if I can make some money," he announces.

After he leaves, Martha pretends not to notice the tense silence among them. Assuming the role of hostess, she explains the menu to Louise and the others.

"They do a remarkable rib eye here," she says. "And I always love the lamb." It's Martha's way of showing she often dines with Dave – and without Louise. The arrow finds its mark. Noting the fleeting look of pain cross Louise's face, Ellen begins to understand what's going on.

They are already seated at their table when Dave returns.

"I just lost $10,000, but don't worry about it," he says, chuckling, with a gambler's bravado, "I'll get it back later this evening."

Martha pats Dave's hand.

"Of course you will," she says a bit loudly.

Louise ignores the gesture and turns to Ellen.

"How was the drive down?" she asks her sister-in-law brightly. "Did you have much traffic on the Parkway?"

During dinner, Dave hardly touches his steak. He seems preoccupied, at least until the subject of his sister, Zelda, comes up. Zelda, seven years younger than Dave, has been in a mental health facility for many years, but now lives with their aging parents in Asbury Park. It's been a perennial topic of discussion for Dave and his brother: Once their parents (now in their 90s) can no longer care for her, how will Dave and Ira step in, and what will they do? At this point, Louise excuses herself to go to the lady's room. After she leaves the table, Martha straightens up in her chair and lays her cards on the table.

"Don't worry," she assures Ira and Ellen. "Dave and I are going to take care of Zelda."

Ira stares at Martha, jaw agape. Ellen, infuriated, hisses to Dave. "How can you be doing this to your wife?" She glares at Martha in disgust.

"Ellen, I love you, but it's none of your business," Dave replies sharply.

For good measure, he directs a withering "don't lecture me" look at Ira. The tension breaks the instant Louise returns to her chair.

"What did I miss?" she asks, smiling.

"We're just discussing dessert!" Martha says, with forced cheer.

In early March, Dave slips up. He writes checks to Resorts totaling $200,000 on the wrong account. When he learns the bank is sending them back, citing insufficient funds, Dave panics. He's terrified that Resorts will cut off his gambling credit line. He immediately calls Gary Grant and tells him of the error. It was his bookkeeper's fault, he tells Grant; "I'm going to fire her for this," he adds. Meanwhile, he assures Grant that he'll bring a certified check to the casino later that day.

Dave then rushes to the correct bank and asks it to issue a certified check to Resorts for the amount due. As Dave hands the check to Grant, he apologizes profusely.

"I've spoken to my bookkeeper and this won't happen again," Dave tells him.

"That's fine, Dave," Grant says with a broad smile. "Thanks for catching it and rectifying it so quickly."

Reading the unspoken anxiety on Dave's face Grant adds quickly, "And this won't affect your credit rating, no worries."

It was the kind of mistake that anyone could make, Grant reasons – and Dave has always been an honorable guy.

That evening, Grant tells Jim Carr the story.

"It seems it was an innocent mix-up and he resolved it in a matter of a couple of hours," Grant tells him. "You should have seen how apologetic he was."

Carr nods. Still, he is starting to wonder about what lies ahead for Dave.

"I've worked in casinos my entire life. In all that time," Carr replies, "I've never seen any gambler play the way Zarin plays now, at such sustained high levels. I just wonder, how long can he keep it up?"

Grant agrees; he's seen firsthand just how aggressively Mr. Z is playing these days.

"Nothing goes on forever," Grant says. "It's just a matter of time before Zarin runs out of money."

But neither man expresses any concern about Zarin crashing and burning.

"Either way, we'll get paid," Grant adds. "Zarin has land and his business generates a lot of money. And he tells me his girlfriend is even more loaded."

Later that night, Carr tells Davis about the returned checks and Zarin's rapid response to the crisis. He echoes Grant's remark that Zarin won't be able to keep gambling at such a high level. Listening in silence to Carr describe the situation, Davis narrows his eyes.

***

Compounding Dave's discomfort these days is his severe and chronic heartburn, which no amount of Maalox seems to help. Dave doesn't connect this physical discomfort to constant stress from his gambling; he's too busy juggling his bank balances to pause and reflect on any other topic. He writes big personal checks to Martha, so she can help him pay off the casino. He's so consumed with chasing the next win that he can't keep track of what he owes and to whom. He has no idea how many checks he is writing or for how much.

When Martha's banks in Montreal alert her that her account balances are low, she rushes to Dave. She demands that he resolve the situation.

"We have to deposit $400,000 to cover these checks!" she exclaims, clearly upset.

"Don't worry, Martha, I have it under control," Dave reassures her, hoping to calm her down.

By now, it's a familiar routine. He cashes in his chips and some non-gaming personal checks, takes the bundles of cash to the bank, exchanges them for a certified check, and hands it over to Martha. She then flies back to Canada to deposit that certified check, which Dave assumes will cover the uncashed personal checks he has written to her. But rather than destroying or returning Dave's personal checks, Martha keeps them tucked away in the envelope in her drawer. Dave doesn't realize she hasn't returned the checks to him. He leaves it up to Martha to handle his cash flow so he can concentrate on playing.

One evening in March, when Jon is in town working on a project, Dave asks him for a favor.

"I'd like you to go to the bank tomorrow morning and make a deposit for me. I have to go back to Elizabeth early, before the banks open."

No problem, Jon thinks. The next morning, at around 7 a.m., Jon goes to Dave's suite, where Dave hands over a bulging manila envelope full of cash. Dutifully, Jon takes the money to the Guarantee Bank in Atlantic City.

"I'd like to deposit this in Mr. David Zarin's account," Jon tells the teller.

"Oh yes, Mr. Zarin's 'daily'." The teller smiles and nods knowingly at the other tellers at the window.

"We can set our watches by the time he shows up each morning with his deposits."

She opens the envelope and shakes stacks of hundred dollar bills onto the counter. Jon's jaw drops at the sight of the growing mound of bills, neatly bundled in Resorts bands. The teller carefully counts the cash in front of him. It takes a while. The final total: $80,000 (about $340,000 today).

It's now the end of March. Dave is exhausted. His eyes are glazed over; he has been playing craps for 15 to 17 hours almost every single day, signing markers totaling $3.3 million (or $14.2 million in today's dollars). He covers his losses by paying Resorts with personal checks totaling $2,521,000 (about $11.9 million in 2024) and cashes non-gaming checks totaling $481,000 (equivalent to $2.3 million today) which he deposits in his bank account.

Martha tells him his uncashed checks to her are piling up again, and she'll feel more secure if he gave her some cash. So he gives her certified checks of $708,000 to deposit in her bank in Canada. The cash infusion into her accounts calms Martha and with her confidence in him restored, she eagerly returns to Atlantic City and her comped life. But, consumed by his singular desire to just keep gambling, he doesn't ask Martha for an accounting of what he actually owes her. He seems to have forgotten about all those older checks he has already reimbursed to her. The only thing that matters to Dave is that Martha is still at his side, wishing him luck and helping him finance his habit.

By mid-April, Dave is careening downhill, with no brakes.

The constant anxiety and chronic heartburn are becoming intolerable. He is nearing complete physical and mental collapse. Finally, he is ready to admit that there's a connection between his personal wellbeing and his gambling; that he can no longer keep things together.

In his hotel suite, he pops another antacid.

"I can't do this anymore," he tells Martha, rubbing his stomach. "This is making me physically ill. I need to stop."

He tells her he plans to go to Jack Davis to discuss his gambling debts to Resorts.

"I am going to tell him that even though I don't know how many checks are out there or how much money is involved, I'll work out payment for all of it. I need to do this. Now. It's the only way I can climb out of this situation."

Martha is furious. She has invested too much in Dave to lose him and their extravagant lifestyle. She glances down at her Piaget watch, caressing its gold band and the diamond-rimmed face.

"You can't do that," she tells him, firmly. "You only need more time."

Dave sits back on the couch, grimacing at the burning sensation in his belly.

"I'm going to Davis;" he says, dully. "This whole thing has to stop."

Martha flies into a rage.

"What are you saying? You can't do that! What's telling Jack Davis going to accomplish?" she shouts.

Martha pulls out what she calculates is her strongest weapon.

"He'll shut down your gambling," she warns him. "You'll be finished."

To escape her harangue, Dave flees to the bathroom, locks the door and slumps down atop the toilet seat, holding his head between his hands. Martha continues railing at Dave through the door, her voice getting louder and louder. She goes on for over two hours as Dave remains silent, hunkered down on the toilet seat. When she eventually stops shouting, Dave slowly stands up and opens the bathroom door. He walks to the couch and lies down, covering his eyes with his arm. Martha calmly perches beside him on the arm of the sofa, and reaches out to stroke his head.

"Look Dave, we can work this out," she says, her voice hoarse from yelling. "You just need more time. But I can't give you any more checks on my Canadian accounts. I'm overdrawn. You'll need to cover these from now on."

"How?" Dave asks despairingly. "I need more time to cover these checks."

"Well, maybe, you should go to Montreal and open your own bank account," Martha suggests.

"Remember that it takes four to six weeks for a check to clear both banking systems. That will give you enough time to cover each check. You wouldn't have to worry about checks being returned for insufficient funds."

Dave is silent for a while, still covering his eyes. He owes so much money!

"Okay." He sighs. "Introduce me to your bankers in Montreal."

Dave and Martha fly to Montreal the next evening, April 16. The morning after that, Dave opens a U.S. dollar bank account at the Royal Bank of Canada with an initial deposit of $10,000. Martha remains in Montreal, but Dave rushes back to Atlantic City to gamble. Returning to Resorts, he immediately heads over to the cage to find Gary Grant. He hands Grant several checks drawn on the Royal Bank of Canada account totaling $180,000.

Grant looks at the checks, puzzled.

"What's this for?" he asks.

"These checks are to cover most of the markers I signed over the past week," he tells Grant. "I opened up an account in Canada, Gary, because I need the additional time to clear my checks."

Grant doesn't say anything as Dave turns and makes a beeline to the comfort of his craps table.

Returning to the cage, Grant calls Matt Kearny, the director of Internal Audit and Control for Resorts with the news that Mr. Z just opened a U.S. dollar bank account in Canada.

Grant tells Kearny that Zarin's girlfriend has used her own Canadian accounts to gamble, so they know it could take Resorts a month or more before they know whether a check is good or will be returned for insufficient funds. Grant then calls Carr and Fiore, the senior VP for finance, to advise them of Zarin's new banking arrangement. They decide to continue extending as much credit to Zarin as he wants.

But the internal discussions continue and Resorts ramps up its scrutiny of Zarin's playing. The next day, Kearny meets with Gore, the executive vice president for finance at Resorts, and tells him that Zarin now is writing checks on a Canadian bank rather than one in New Jersey – and why he is doing so. Martha's 'smart' solution has backfired: It has put all the top executives of Resorts on high alert about Zarin's credit and his ability to make good on any gambling debts. They all recognize in Mr. Z the signs of a gambler spinning out of control. Still, no one suggests restoring the guardrails.

Dave gambles every day in April. Sometimes, he spends 17 hours daily at the craps table, taking barely enough time to eat, nap and shower before starting over again. Around this time, Dave also begins to put $2,000 on several high-risk, high-return one-roll bets that will pay off if the dice produce a specific duplicate number or hit the numbers 2, 3, 11 or 12. The result is that he now has about $30,000 (equivalent to more than $140,000 in today's dollars) on the craps table at each roll of the dice. A capacity crowd of awestruck gamblers surrounds the craps table, some craning their necks, to watch the spectacle. Dave remains a big draw, to the delight of Resorts' managers. He signs an ever-increasing number of markers to keep the dice rolling.

Ironically, as the casino continues to enable Dave's manic gambling, Resorts' hotel hosts a four-day conference several floors above the casino. The topic? Compulsive gambling, a problem that both the gaming industry and society at large are only beginning to acknowledge. Johns Hopkins University's Compulsive Gambling Counseling Center is less than a year old. The center's head, Robert Poltzer, the key speaker at the conference, tells attendees that gambling is an impulse control disorder that afflicts more than a million Americans, 40,000 of whom live in New Jersey. He then offers a sober warning to the conference goers. "The numbers will mushroom as the crowds flock to Atlantic City."

Poltzer doesn't know that just downstairs, he could watch a living example of this trend and the terrible hold that addictive gaming can have on someone. Glued to his spot at the craps table, Dave hits big on his number. A wave of euphoria washes over him as the crowd erupts into cheers.

***

On Monday, April 21, Grant tells Kearny that Zarin was TTO'ed for $800,000 in credit over the weekend. Kearny calls Gore; they decide to ask the Royal Bank of Canada to expedite the processing of Zarin's checks. The next step is for Kearney and Tom O'Donnell, Resorts' treasurer, to call RBC with their request. A week later, Grant notifies Kearny that Zarin opened yet *another* Canadian bank account, this time at the Bank of Nova Scotia. Zarin had signed another $800,000 in markers and wrote personal checks of $800,000 on this second bank account over this past weekend. He also writes an additional $360,000 in non-gaming personal checks over the same weekend.

The next day, Kearny, Resorts' head of internal audit, meets with Davis at a conference in Miami.

"Well, our favorite high-roller has opened a Canadian bank account to extend the period for clearing his checks," Kearny tells Davis. "And he's already written a significant number of large personal checks against the account."

Davis' eyebrows arch in surprise.

"But there's more," Kearney adds. "He just opened a *second* Canadian bank account and is already writing several personal checks on that account, too."

Now Davis is worried. "This is getting out of hand," he tells Kearny. "Let's organize a call with the team so I can get a full picture of the situation."

Davis, Kearney, Carr, Grant, Fiore, and Pete Burns all participate in the conference call, together with the director of casino accounting, and Gallion, the assistant cage manager. Davis gets straight to the point.

"Someone please tell me how many personal checks Zarin has given to us recently?" he asks the group.

It's up to Gallion to deliver the bad news. "More than 50 from his Canadian accounts in the last two weeks."

"That's not all," Gallion adds. "He's also signed markers during the month of April totaling $6.5 million" ($30.7 million in today's dollars).

Someone on the call gives a low whistle; no one speaks for a few seconds. It's Davis who breaks the silence.

"Okay, you need to talk to him about these checks and the Canadian bank account," Davis tells Grant. "And I think you should consider cutting off his credit."

In spite of the staggering amounts, some members of the Resorts team balk at this measure.

"That's a pretty drastic step, don't you think?" Carr interjects. "I mean, if we do that, we risk having Zarin jumping over to the Regency, or some other casino."

Another long silence follows.

"Then, Jim, you and Gary, go talk some sense to him." Davis exhales. He then reconsiders.

"No, wait. Forget it. Rip the Band-Aid off. Tell him we're not extending any more credit to him."

***

Carr and Grant lie in wait to catch Dave on his way to the craps table on the morning of April 30. They take him to the coffee shop and sit down.

"Dave, we're now able to expedite the processing of your Canadian checks through a courier system," Carr tells him. "It now takes us only three days to clear each check, and we're seeing some of the checks coming back to us."

Dave blanches. "But I need more than a three-day clearance process to cover them," he protests.

"We know," Carr says. "And we have decided – reluctantly – to cut off your credit line for the time being. Only until we can clear up this matter."

Dave isn't comforted by Carr's regretful tone or his attempts to reassure him.

"We just need a time-out, to catch things up," Carr adds. "We really like you. We know you're an honorable guy and you're our most valuable customer. But we have no choice."

Dave quickly absorbs the implications of this decision. He grits his teeth, seething.

"You can't do that!" he exclaims. "I can't gamble without a credit line. You're shutting me down!"

His anger tailing off; Dave adopts an almost-pleading tone.

"You're not giving me a chance to get even," he says, imploringly.

Dave turns to Grant, to appeal against this ultimatum from Resorts.

"Gary, are you going along with this? I thought we were friends!"

Grant lowers his eyes and says nothing.

"We're very sorry," Carr continues. "We'll work through this as quickly as possible so you can get back to the craps tables as soon as possible."

Carr and Grant stand up and walk away, leaving Dave sitting alone, stunned and dazed. His mouth is dry, he feels his heart pounding in his chest; his breathing comes in short gasps. His whole world has screeched to a stop. Without craps, what is he going to do? He sits at the café table, his head in his hands, trying to calm himself down. After a while, he gets up slowly, and walks back to his room.

Back in his suite, Dave stands at the window, and gazes at the ocean waves pounding the beach. He watches them rise, crest, then pull back, only to rise again. Relentless. Like the continual throw of the dice. Dave is suddenly overwhelmed by a feeling of despair. What is he doing?!!

Dave picks up the phone to call Rich, Jon and me and asks us to come to Atlantic City that evening for an emergency meeting. We agree to meet in his hotel suite at 7 p.m. I drop everything and drive to Atlantic City from Washington. Rich makes the trip from Harrisburg, and Jon drives down from Trenton. While none of us knows for sure what this emergency involves, we're each certain that it's somehow linked to his gambling.

Dave then calls Martha in Montreal. He's panicking again, and finds himself short of breath when she answers the call.

"Resorts just cut off my credit line," he tells her. "They're expediting the clearing of my checks, and some are being returned for insufficient funds—"

"Wait, what? When? What did they say?" Martha asks sharply.

"I'm so upset!" Dave continues, ignoring her questions. "I, I won't have the time to clear all of these checks! And I won't be able to win back my losses. I don't know what to do!"

"Dave, Dave, you have to calm down," Martha says, evenly. "We can fix this." Martha can't imagine their joy ride may be over.

"Martha, we have to resolve this quickly and without any publicity," Dave blurts out. Martha agrees.

"It's okay, Dave. You're their best customer," she reassures him, determined to keep him focused. "They'll want to work out a payment schedule. Then we'll be able to continue, just like before."

"I don't know, I don't know," he mumbles. "I need to talk with Davis, to resolve this."

"Do you want me to come back to Atlantic City?" Martha asks, as if soothing a child.

"I'll let you know after I speak with Davis."

Rich, Jon and I arrive that evening around 7 p.m., within 10 minutes of each other, to find Dave pacing the room, his shirt rumpled and tie askew, beads of sweat on his face. The three of us sit in a row on the couch in the living room and Dave turns to face us, still standing.

"Guys, I am in a lot of trouble," he confesses, his voice shaking. "I've lost a lot of money. I don't really know how much yet. Maybe everything I have. Everything I expect to have. More than I can repay."

"What?" I blurt out. We glance at each other in shock. It's even worse than we imagined.

Dave is speaking quickly, without pausing for breath.

"The casino just cut off my credit. I need to get this back under control. It'll take a while to work through this problem. I need to pay back the casino as soon as I can. I hope this won't hurt the business, but I can't be sure."

Rich drops his head into his hands.

"Oh God," he says in despair.

"How much did you lose, Dad?" I ask.

The answer is horrifying. "I don't really know," he says.

My voice rises, even as I struggle to hang on to the last of my calm. "Did you lose one million dollars, or two million? Give us an approximate number."

Dave shakes his head. "It's a lot more than that," he replies.

"More than *two million*?" Rich asks, jumping up, shocked. "Do you even *have* more money than that?"

The room is silent.

"I think it might be closer to $10 or $15 million," Dave admits, haltingly.

Rich slowly sinks back onto the sofa. All three of us are frozen on that big Sinatra suite couch. Time stands still; I have to remind myself to breathe.

"You. Lost. 10. To. 15. Million. Dollars," I repeat, with incredulity. "You don't *have* that much money to lose," I add, my tone rising as anger sets in.

Dave nods, "I know, I know," his voice breaking. "That's why I am in so much trouble. Some of my checks are starting to bounce."

Another shocked silence.

Then Rich asks, hesitantly, "how many checks?"

Dave shakes his head. "I don't know. I don't know how many checks or how much money I wrote on these checks." He squeezes his eyes shut in pain. "It could be 50 or more checks. It could be millions of dollars."

I feel a wave of nausea as I force myself to take another deep breath and ask him, "Dad, writing checks without sufficient funds to cover them is illegal. Is that what you did?"

Dave cast his eyes downward. "I, I don't know. Maybe," he mumbles. Then he raises his head and looks me in the eyes. "Yes, yes, I guess I did," he replies grimly.

"How much money, how many checks?" I press. But Dave still can't answer.

"I don't know. I don't know. I didn't keep records," he says in anguish. "We will see over the next two weeks how many checks are returned." He switches his focus for a moment to another big worry. "If this situation leaks out to the public, I'll never be able to develop another project."

At this point, we have no idea if this is going to hurt his business. There's still a lot we don't know about the extent of Dave's debt, or the depths of his compulsion.

But what we do know is that Dave's gambling days are over and his business may be finished.

CHAPTER 8: LOSING CONTROL

Rich, Jon and I leave Dave's suite in a daze after his two-hour confession. We ride the elevator down in silence, heading for the casino bar, although we all know that no amount of alcohol will dull the shock. We sit at a table, oblivious to the cacophony of chiming slot machines, spinning roulette wheels, and cheering gamblers. Had anyone asked us to guess at a worst-case scenario, we might have calculated that, just maybe, Dave had gambled away $2 million. That kind of loss would be catastrophic; it would likely swallow all of his assets. But the monstrous scenario Dave described is beyond belief. How did we fail to realize how dire things had become?

In retrospect, it's hard to see what we could have done to head off this catastrophe. Dave convinced himself that he had control over his gambling activities, behavior that's typical of a compulsive gambler. We didn't recognize or understand it, either. But even if we had, Dave is a force of nature, he's unstoppable. Only the casino had the power to stop Dave, but as long as it profited from his obsession, it wasn't in its interest to apply the brakes.

The day after Dave admits to us what had happened, he begins a series of meetings with Resorts officials to figure out how to resolve the matter as quietly – and quickly – as possible. Resorts officials, for their part, share Dave's objective, but their reasons are quite different.

Their New Jersey casino license is up for renewal and they can't afford any negative news or allegations of violations of the gaming regulations to become public.

Dave's first meeting is with Jack Davis and the Resorts' general counsel, Charles Murphy. Murphy tells Dave they will conduct a thorough accounting to be sure that Dave and Martha haven't been involved in a skimming operation. The casino wants to be sure that they weren't taking money out of the casino for any other reason than to pay the casino debts, and to verify that they weren't sharing any of that stolen money with Resorts executives who might have conspired with them.

"You can bet that the Division of Gaming Enforcement is going to look very closely at the possibility of collaboration." Murphy explains. "So Resorts will do its own investigation in advance, and you need to meet with their internal auditor, Matt Kearney. He'll review all the checks you and Martha wrote and trace them all back to the casino. Nobody wants any surprises."

Dave agrees immediately.

"I intend to repay all of our debts and I'll have enough funds to pay you back in full, though not right away," he says. "Until then, I have collateral to protect you."

But actually, Dave already is effectively insolvent; he just doesn't realize it yet. His liabilities far exceed his assets. While he still retains stakes in several projects in the pipeline or under development, those projects won't generate any significant revenue until they're completed.

Dave asks Martha to come to Atlantic City and together they meet with Resorts' accountants. They spend two days reviewing every check Dave and Martha wrote to Resorts since he began gambling there nearly two years ago.

By early June, when the dust settles and all the checks that have insufficient funds are returned, it becomes clear just how out of control Dave had become. The numbers tell the story: Dave and Martha signed and/or wrote markers, personal checks and non-gaming checks totaling $14,698,000 (equivalent to over $69.5 million in 2024) in the three-month period from February to April 1980. Of this amount, Dave paid $10,038,000 (equivalent to over $47.5 million today). But checks totaling $4,660,000 (over $22 million in today's dollars) were returned for insufficient funds, almost all of them written between April 17 and April 29. A period of only 12 days!

In that three-month period, Dave cashed non-gaming personal checks totaling $1,771,000 and Martha cashed non-gaming checks totaling $246,000. Dave's credit limit reached $3,076,000 (or about $14.5 million today) although his reference card reflects that he maintained an "official" credit balance of only $305,000. The difference between those two amounts represented the informal TTO arrangement that the casino's top executives had green-lighted only months earlier to keep their high roller returning to the tables. Resorts also extended to Martha a credit limit of $1,225,000 ($5.8 million today); well above the $240,000 maximum noted on her credit reference card.

Over that same three month time frame, Dave deposited more than $7,350,000 ($34.7 million today) in cash at the Guarantee Bank in Atlantic City and bought a total of $2,271,000 ($10.7 million today) in certified checks from the Guarantee Bank, most of which he gave to Martha to cover the checks she wrote on her Canadian accounts. In effect, Dave was continuously cycling cash to cover checks that he previously had written.

Together, Dave and Martha now owe Resorts $4,660,000. Dave's returned checks represent $3,435,000 of this amount, while Martha owes another $1,225,000. Most of Martha's debt involves checks that she wrote and on which she stopped payment after Resorts cut off Dave's credit. Dave also has unpaid markers at Regency, the Caesar's-owned casino down the street, totaling $250,000. Martha owes Regency another $200,000 for unpaid markers.

Now that Dave understands the extent of the financial chaos, he turns his attention to negotiating a settlement. He schedules another meeting with Jack Davis for June 9, only to realize that he won't be able to offer much in the way of collateral to Resorts, because Martha has first call on most of those assets. He confesses this to Murphy, who sighs in exasperation.

"Resorts can't begin negotiating a settlement with you until Mrs. Nemtin releases her security interest in your assets," Murphy tells Dave.

His meeting with Jack Davis is scheduled to take place the next morning. Dave wants to hammer out a deal, so he needs to convince Martha to release her security interests in his assets. He raises the subject with her over dinner. He also asks Jon to draw up a release document and bring it to his suite first thing the next morning. Dave is so worried about keeping his gambling losses under wraps that he directs Jon not to tell Weintraub, the lawyer who represented Martha when the original agreement was drawn up. The clock is ticking; Dave needs to take Martha's signed release to his morning meeting with Davis.

Jon arrives at 9 a.m. to find Dave and Martha having breakfast. Jon pulls the release agreement out of his briefcase for her to sign.

"I've explained to Martha that she needs to sign this release so we can settle our debt with the casino," Dave says, glancing at Martha.

Putting down her coffee cup, Martha takes the document. As she begins to read, she frowns slightly, and hesitates.

Dave reaches across the table to touch her hand gently.

"This is really urgent, Martha. I have to take this to Davis in an hour." He gives her hand a light squeeze. "This release means that you and I will be able to resolve all our outstanding debt to Resorts and be free of it.

"We discussed this with Charley Murphy," he continues, patiently. "Their position is that you need to release your collateral before they can begin any discussions to resolve this matter."

Martha nods and reviews the document slowly, considering each word carefully. She wants to help Dave to settle with Resorts, but asks Jon questions about what happens if Dave doesn't reach an agreement with the casino. The answers clearly don't reassure her.

"This isn't good enough," she declares, looking up at Jon. "I want some language spelling out that if there's no settlement with Resorts, I'll get my collateral back."

Dave agrees to the change.

"I'm happy to work on the wording, but Martha, you need to understand that I am not giving you legal advice," Jon says.

Jon and Martha hammer out the wording of an amendment, which Jon then adds to the drafted agreement by hand. If Dave can't reach a deal with Resorts, the amendment promises that he'll give Martha "a security interest in his properties and the release will be null and void."

Both Dave and Martha sign the release.

Less than an hour later, Dave, Martha and Jon arrive at Jack Davis's office. There they find themselves sitting across the table from Jack, Marvin Ashner, president of the Resorts hotel operation, Jim Carr, Bob Fiore and Matt Kearny. Their goal: to begin discussing payments to be made by Dave and the security to be provided. It's a friendly meeting; both sides expect to wrap up the whole mess promptly.

One by one, they check off items on their list. Kearny confirms that he's accounted for all of Dave and Martha's checks and that he is confident that no skimming took place. Dave tells Davis that Martha has released her collateral; he describes his projects and some of the assets that could serve as collateral. Dave tells Davis he'll give Resorts an interest in all of his projects and turn over the revenue from these projects.

"I'll give this to you to pay off this debt, that is, Mrs. Nemtin's debt and my debt."

Davis, satisfied with how things are going so far, calls Murphy and asks him to immediately begin legal discussions with Dave and his attorneys.

"Let's get this matter behind us," Davis says.

The meeting ends on an upbeat note. A speedy, amicable settlement seems to be a slam dunk. Then reality intervenes.

Several days later, Martha calls Weintraub to tell him that she signed a document releasing her collateral. She tells Dave that Weintraub is upset that she didn't check with him before doing anything.

After the meetings with Resorts, Dave heads home to Elizabeth to tell Louise what has happened. He's dreading the conversation; he's afraid Louise will leave him. In spite of his long-running affair with Martha, he still needs Louise; not only does he still love her, but he depends on her. Louise has always been the anchor of the family. Hopefully, she'll still be willing to serve that role; to understand and forgive him.

When he opens the front door, Dave's immediately enveloped by the familiar aromas wafting from Louise's kitchen. As always, she greets him with a kiss on the cheek. He catches a whiff of her favorite perfume; she's wearing a dress he's admired before. Dave realizes that she's made an extra effort to welcome him home. His throat tightens in shame. Other emotions follow, a conflicting torrent of relief, fear, regret, and yes, love. Over dinner, Dave distractedly picks at his steak. He's sweating; too anxious about talking to Louise to eat the meal she has prepared for him.

Laying down his utensils, Dave clears his throat.

"Louise, I have something to tell you; it's going to be upsetting, but just know now that I can fix it," he opens his confession. He swallows and continues.

"I owe money to Resorts. They've cut off my credit line and stopped me from playing until I can pay them back."

Dave pauses to study Louise's face, which registers confusion, anxiety, and then – finally – anger.

"How...how much do you owe them?" she asks haltingly.

Dave takes a deep breath.

"It's about $4.5 million."

Louise's jaw drops and her fork clatters to the floor.

Dave rushes to fill the silence with an explanation.

"I'm negotiating a settlement with them, which should take about a month or two to resolve. I'm going to get this all behind me quickly. It shouldn't affect my business, and it shouldn't affect our family."

"Four and a half million! Are you insane?" Louise touches the diamond ring she put on expressly for this dinner with Dave.

"Again and again, we find ourselves on this roller coaster, thanks to your risk taking and gambling," she says through gritted teeth. "But never, *never,* has it been this bad. What were you thinking?"

Louise grips the table edge with both hands, as if to hold herself upright.

"You've ruined us," she tells Dave, angrily. "We don't have that kind of money."

"You're overreacting, Louise," Dave insists, trying to calm her. "The business is doing fine, I'll make the money back and can fix this."

"Four and a half million dollars gone, by *gambling!*" Louise says incredulously. "How can that be! You're crazy. How could you let this happen?"

Dave's taken aback. Not only is Louise openly venting

her anger, but she's described his passion for gambling as some kind of mental illness.

"I am not crazy," Dave answers defiantly. "That's not true. I just got carried away and things got out of control. But I'm going to fix it. I can settle with Resorts and get back on track."

Louise is still gripping the table, her knuckles turning white.

"Dave, what planet do you live on?" she demands. "You've lost all of the money you worked so hard for, and now we're deep in debt. And for what?"

Dave stares at his plate in silence.

After a brief pause, Louise continues.

"As I said, Dave, you're sick. Gambling is an obsession, and now it's ruined us."

Dave is growing angrier. "I am not sick. I just need to straighten things out with Resorts and it'll all work out fine in the end."

Louise tilts her head with skepticism. "Throughout our marriage, with all of the ups and downs you have had in business and in gambling, you've somehow managed to land on your feet. But not this time. Not likely. You've gone too far this time."

She pushes back her chair from the table, stands up, marches to their bedroom and slams the door behind her. As soon as she sits down on the bed, her anger changes into fear.

What will become of them?

Louise is too shocked to cry.

***

Despite his strained relationship with Louise, Dave now stays mostly in Elizabeth and works out of his offices in Elizabeth and Harrisburg. While he still has access to his suite at Resorts, it's too painful to stay there as long as he is banned from playing in the casino. Without the excitement from gambling, he's falling into a deep funk. He is obsessed with resolving the matter with Resorts before the news gets out and hurts his business.

Though he's sworn off gambling, Dave hasn't given up Martha. Instead, he invites her to join him when he goes to California to tell his West Coast partners about his situation with Resorts. Dave and Martha stay at the Beverly Hills Hotel for a few days, but it's hardly a romantic interlude like their tryst at the Plaza the year before. Martha constantly harps on the money she believes Dave owes her, and is having serious second thoughts about signing a document relinquishing her security interest in his projects.

Dave's meeting with his partners doesn't go well, either. Their initial response is to terminate the partnership; Dave manages to persuade them to stick with him for at least the next several months. In return they demand that he give them constant updates on the progress of negotiations with Resorts.

Dave returns to his office in Elizabeth. Jon, who is at the office for some meetings, receives a disturbing phone call.

"Mr. Epstein, my name is Peter Trebeco; I'm a special agent with the Federal Bureau of Investigation in Trenton," the caller says. "I'm investigating the situation that occurred between your client, Mr. Zarin, and Resorts, and the monies Mr. Zarin owes the casino."

Jon, alarmed, listens in silence. What 'situation' is this guy talking about?

"I'm authorized to tell you that if Mr. Zarin gives us the names of the casino executives involved in his scheme, we are prepared to make a very favorable deal with Mr. Zarin," the FBI agent explains, calmly.

Jon is floored by the implication.

"I don't understand," he says. "Can you explain precisely what you're asking?"

"Well, we don't believe that Mr. Zarin's cash-skimming scheme to steal money from the casino could have occurred without the involvement of one or more casino executives," Trebeco says. "If he tells us who they are, we are prepared to make a deal with your client."

"I– I think you are misreading this situation here," Jon stammers. "I'm not able to talk right now."

After hanging up, Jon rushes over to Dave in his office and, clearly rattled, recounts the gist of the FBI agent's call.

"The only way the FBI and others are going to understand what really happened is if you acknowledge that you are a compulsive gambler," Jon says. "That you have an illness."

Dave is appalled. An illness? First Louise, and now Jon?

"I am *not* a compulsive gambler!" Dave bellows, still in denial. "You're wrong. I was *never* out of control."

161

Dave's reaction shocks Jon into silence. After everything that has happened, the frenzied gambling, the huge debt, the unraveling of his business and his partnerships, Dave needs to accept the reality that he is addicted to gambling. That is, if he's to have any chance of avoiding prison, much less getting his business back on track.

Now that the FBI is involved, Rich, Jon and I urge Dave to hire a senior lawyer with experience with white-collar criminal cases. Jon already has made some inquiries and recommends Jonathan Goldstein. He served as U.S. attorney for New Jersey and has been an outspoken opponent of the referenda that brought Resorts and its rivals to Atlantic City. Now he's a partner in an eight-attorney law firm in Newark.

Dave and Jon meet with Goldstein and his partner Bob Raymar in their offices, decorated and furnished like a traditional white-shoe firm. They meet in a conference room with a long wooden table, leather seats, and an expansive window overlooking Newark; Manhattan's skyscrapers glint in the distance. Goldstein, 39 years old, is a studious looking man with wire rim glasses and exudes a gravitas that impresses Dave. Over the course of the next hour Dave recounts everything that led up to that day when Resorts pulled the rug out from underneath him: The betting, the money lost and won, Resorts' eagerness to grant his requests for more and more credit, and the resulting debt.

"Now that I'm in this mess, I want to dig myself out as soon as possible and pay what I owe," Dave says. He chokes up, a stricken look appears on his face. "If this gets out to the media I'll be ruined."

When Dave finishes, Goldstein takes a deep breath. Before he responds, he takes a minute to absorb everything that Dave has said, tapping his index finger against the rim of his coffee cup. Seeing that it's empty, Goldstein walks over to the carafe for a refill, gazes out the window, and comes back to the table.

"Dave, I'm struggling to understand your story, and what you want to accomplish," Goldstein tells him bluntly. He pauses. "Do you realize that you're a compulsive gambler?"

Dave sits bolt upright in his chair. "I'm not so sure that's true," he replies, tilting his chin upward and glaring at Goldstein.

While neither Jon, nor members of Dave's family had been able to come up with an effective response to Dave's denials, Goldstein does so handily.

"Well, let me tell you, Dave: you *are* a compulsive gambler," Goldstein says, taking another sip of coffee. "Now, I am not a psychiatrist and I rarely ever gamble. But it doesn't take a psychiatrist to recognize your condition."

Goldstein then fires off a series of questions at Dave.

"Be honest here: Were you gambling out of control during the last four months you played craps at the casino?"

"Yes," Dave answers.

"Did you gamble 15 to 17 hours each day, virtually every day, for four months?"

"Well, yes."

"Did you have an absolute urge, a compulsion to gamble, to get to the craps table?"

Dave nods reluctantly.

"Did you have any idea how much money you were betting?"

"Not really,"

"Was your overriding desire to keep gambling no matter what, and to keep covering your checks to keep gambling, no matter what?"

"Yes," Dave answers, hanging his head.

"Well, Dave," Goldstein spreads his arms open. "I don't know what *you* would call it. I would call it a compulsion to gamble."

Dave leans back, sinking into the chair's plush upholstery. As he processes what Goldstein just said, he gazes out the windows and watches the clouds float past the skyscrapers in the far distance. For the first time, he ponders everything that people have been trying to tell him for months. His own family, Jon, and even Gary Grant. Now Goldstein is saying the same thing, and he's not tiptoeing around it either.

Dave shamefacedly begins to consider, for the first time, that maybe he wasn't in control after all. Still, the notion that he has been in the grip of some kind of addiction frightens and repulses him. Instinctively, he rejects the idea that gambling could be like heroin or cocaine or something that impaired his judgment. He feels his stomach turn into knots.

But Goldstein is just warming up.

"Now, Dave, tell me this," he continues, "did Resorts know that you were gambling every day, 15 to 17 hours each day, and that you were betting over $22,000 on each roll of the dice?"

"Yes, of course they did," Dave says, perplexed by the question.

"Did Resorts know how much credit they were feeding you to be able to gamble?" Goldstein asks.

"Sure," Dave replies; certainly, he and Grant had had lots of conversations about credit and Dave's impatience with the limits.

"Did Resorts know how many markers you were signing and the total amount of the markers?"

Dave is bemused. "Of course,"

"Did Resorts know how much money you were losing each month?"

Dave nods.

"Did Resorts know that you were leaving the casino with tens of thousands of dollars every few days?" Goldstein asks.

"Sure. After all, their staff handed me rolls of hundreds and watched me walk out the door with them."

"Did Resorts know that all of the credit they gave Martha was for your use?"

"They handed me her chips to play," Dave says.

Goldstein delivers his verdict. "Then, Dave, you certainly have responsibility for what transpired," he declares. "And you may face substantial consequences for your part in it. But –"

Another pause. "But don't you think Resorts also has some responsibility for what happened to you?"

Dave's eyes widen at this novel concept.

"Isn't this a little like a bar owner giving unlimited alcohol to an alcoholic?" asks Goldstein, rhetorically. "Certainly, if I can figure out during this single meeting that you're a compulsive gambler, the casino knew that too – and they have known it for a long time."

Dave stares down at the conference table. Goldstein is framing his situation in a whole new way and Dave struggles to follow the attorney's logic.

"What are you saying?" Dave asks him. "What are you recommending?"

Goldstein leans over the table, making eye contact.

"I'm suggesting that maybe you shouldn't be so ready to pay Resorts in full; that maybe they are to blame, too, and should share some of the pain. We should consider all of these facts in deciding what to do."

Goldstein lays out his proposed legal approach. It's a scorched earth strategy. Goldstein wants to go after Resorts hard to get the leverage to reach a far more favorable settlement. He thinks Resorts can't stand the heat of such a battle with the regulators watching every detail.

Jon worries that hardball may not be necessary; may, in fact, be overkill. After all, Resorts is much less worried about the monetary losses than about the prospect of losing its casino license. The executives there just want a fast, quiet settlement; something that will satisfy the Division of Gaming Enforcement. Dave also desperately wants a quick, quiet settlement to avoid any bad publicity. Since Resorts and Dave really have the same objective, Jon warns Dave privately that Goldstein's approach may be needlessly contentious. Nevertheless, Goldstein makes a persuasive case for assigning some culpability for all this to

Resorts. That gives Dave food for thought, and convinces him that it might be worthwhile to see if he can escape the mess with a better deal.

But it quickly becomes clear that Dave and Resorts won't end up settling everything as quietly and amicably as everyone had originally hoped and expected. Goldstein, Jon and the Resorts lawyers hold their meeting at Charles Murphy's law firm in New York. Facing the three of them are Murphy and his partners, flanked by a collection of young attorneys and note takers.

Murphy, a graying, seasoned lawyer in his mid-sixties kicks off the discussion genially enough, expressing his hope and expectation that the parties can quickly reach a settlement. He informs Goldstein and Jon that the investigation by the Division of Gaming Enforcement is in the document-gathering phase, and that they will be closely scrutinizing any settlement between Resorts and Zarin. He wraps up by telling everyone that his comments are "just between us girls in the room."

Goldstein, acting like the dour former U.S. Attorney he is, replies sharply. "There is *nothing* just between us girls in this room."

A chill instantly falls over the group. Murphy is a deal guy, a fixer. The last thing he wants is confrontation. He's looking to craft a smooth, pragmatic solution. Goldstein's adversarial, almost prosecutorial posture strikes a sour note. The mood in the room becomes increasingly tense.

Nevertheless, both sides embark on a series of intensive biweekly meetings and frequent conference calls. Over the next several months, they exchange multiple drafts of possible settlements. It's a painstaking, protracted negotiation. Eventually, the lawyers hammer out an agreement that would require Dave to hand over to Resorts a 15% ownership stake in the Marina Towers project. That is all that Dave has the authority to transfer without his partners' consent. Since the project is still in development, there's no guarantee that it will be as valuable as Dave expects it to be and as Resorts calculates it could be. Under the circumstances, the settlement is a good deal for Dave. The lawyers shake hands and expect both sides will agree to sign.

After one of the first peaceful nights' sleep he's had in months, Dave wakes up in the Sinatra suite feeling refreshed. He showers, shaves and orders a hearty breakfast before heading off to a meeting with Jack Davis to confirm the deal. Dave feels as if a giant boulder has just rolled off his back.

While Dave is breakfasting in his suite, Jack Davis is on the phone filling in his New Jersey gaming lawyer, Joel Sterns, on the details of the final agreement. Joel hadn't been involved in the negotiations, and he isn't happy with the results.

"Jack, this is a terrible deal. It's a non-starter for Resorts," Sterns says. "The Division of Gaming Enforcement is going to be examining this settlement with a microscope. And they aren't going to be satisfied. They'll expect Resorts to get more than a single project's revenue that might or might not materialize, and to hold security in *all* of Zarin's assets."

Davis is surprised and irritated.

"Joel, I don't care how much money we get from Dave or what assets they're secured with," he retorts. "I'm worried about our license renewal. That's worth *hundreds of millions* of dollars to us."

Davis concedes that the Division of Gaming Enforcement will be all over the deal, but adds "I'm most worried about them slapping us with credit violations." Wrapping up the Zarin deal now might prevent that, he argues.

"I understand," Sterns says. "But the settlement has to look like a good deal for Resorts. Not just to the Division of Gaming Enforcement and the Casino Control Commission, but to the press, too. And if this gets out…"

Sterns doesn't need to finish his thought. There's no way that Resorts can afford the perception that Resorts agreed to a sweetheart settlement of Dave's debt.

Davis hangs up the phone with a sigh. Here we go again, he thinks to himself.

Soon after, Dave arrives at Davis' office, and is surprised to find him looking glum rather than pleased.

"I'm sorry, Dave. We can't accept this deal," Davis says. He quickly recounts his conversation with Joel Sterns.

Dave fights back the anxiety welling up inside his chest. Immediately, he tells Davis that he's willing to hand over his interest in all of his assets if that's what it takes to settle matters.

"Go talk to the lawyers," Davis says. Dave turns to the door.

"Oh, and Dave, we need you to vacate the Sinatra suite in the next few days," Davis adds quietly. "I hope you understand."

Dave's shoulders sag. He nods silently.

But while he's packing up his belongings in the sun-filled suite, Dave hears from Goldstein, who advises against handing over his interest in all his assets.

"If you can be patient, we can resurrect the original deal with just a little sweetening," he counsels his client. Dave wavers; he has a sinking feeling that his woes are far from over. But he decides to go with Goldstein's advice. The negotiations go back to square one.

Dave spends most of the summer in Elizabeth, going to Atlantic City only for critical meetings about his projects or for negotiations with Resorts. His perpetual state of anxiety is crippling. Martha, even though she's back in Montreal, isn't helping. Dave has deliberately kept her out of the negotiations, but they talk on the phone almost daily to discuss where everything stands. Inevitably Martha gets around to repeating her claim that Dave still owes her $3 million for all of the money she advanced to him. Dave tries to avoid confrontation, but finally he snaps.

"Give me a break, Martha!" he tells her on one of their calls. "I don't owe you all that." Even if he agreed with her assessment, he adds, "I can't do anything about what I owe you until we resolve everything with Resorts." By October, with no settlement in sight, Resorts is under great pressure from the Division of Gaming Enforcement and the Casino Control Commission to sue Dave if matters aren't resolved very soon. Resorts continues to demand full payment of Dave's obligations and his guarantee of the proceeds from several of his projects under development. Goldstein, meanwhile, sticks to his recommendation that Dave take a hard line.

"Resorts needs to shoulder some of the responsibility for this mess, too." he tells Dave.

"In my opinion, the gambling debt is unenforceable as a matter of law under the New Jersey Casino Control Act. Resorts violated many casino regulations to extend credit to you. They're not blameless."

Although Dave is anxious to settle, he continues to defer to Goldstein and agrees to his strategy.

A month later, with matters still up in the air, Joel Sterns calls Martha at her apartment in Montreal.

"Listen, Martha, I'm telling you right now – and you had better tell Dave – that I have an action ready on my desk to go and I'm going to file it with the court if Dave doesn't finally agree to settle."

Now it's Joel's turn to play hardball, and Martha is terrified. As soon as she hangs up, she calls Dave, hysterical.

"I thought you were going to settle all of this? Why is the Resorts lawyer calling me?" Martha shrieks.

Dave lets her vent for a few more minutes, then calmly tells her that Goldstein thinks it's a bad deal and advises him not to settle. As for Joel Sterns? "He's just bluffing, don't worry," Dave tells her.

A couple of weeks later, Sterns delivers an equally ominous message to Jon, leaving it on his answering machine.

"We're filing this lawsuit because we have to do it," he says. "We don't have a choice, but we still really want to resolve things with you guys."

The axe falls the next day, when Resorts follows through on its threats. The casino files a civil complaint against Dave and Martha in New Jersey State Court. The suit, alleging that they both defrauded the casino, claims that Dave owes Resorts $3,435,000 and Martha a total of $1,225,000.

The legal action throws Dave into a tailspin; he's terrified that news of the lawsuit and Resorts' allegations will hit the papers. Despite his client's mounting anxiety, Goldstein insists on staying the course. He recommends that Dave file a countersuit in federal court against Resorts and its officials personally.

Two weeks later, Goldstein follows through. On Dave's behalf, he files a civil lawsuit against Resorts, as well as Crosby, Davis and seven other Resorts employees, alleging they violated the Racketeer Influenced and Corrupt Organization (RICO) Act. Specifically, the countersuit claims that Resorts acted illegally when it extended credit to Dave. The casino's goal, it alleges, was to induce him to rack up a substantial gambling debt so it could acquire his real estate interests.

Goldstein goes further, claiming on Dave's behalf that Resorts violated the New Jersey casino credit law in numerous ways. Goldstein draws on the knowledge he acquired during his longstanding battle to keep casinos out of the state as well on his concerns about gambling addiction when he asserts in the complaint that Resorts has a duty to exercise care and restraint in extending credit. The icing on the cake? Resorts, Goldstein claims, intentionally violated its duty to a gambling patron whom it knew to be a compulsive gambler.

Goldstein wants to get Resorts' attention. He succeeds beyond his wildest expectations. Not only does he place the issue of gambling addiction at the heart of a ground-breaking lawsuit, but by framing it as a RICO civil suit, a jury can award Dave three times the amount of damages and attorney fees.

I help draft the complaint. If we prevail, for the first time a court will hold a casino responsible for improper conduct in extending credit to a compulsive gambler. We know this could set an important precedent nationwide. Though I think Goldstein's RICO claim is over the top, I see the casino's behavior as clearly having been unconscionable. Resorts had to have recognized Dave's compulsive gambling. Instead, they stood by calmly, watching him rack up one loss after another, play for a dozen hours or more a day. Far from reining him in, Resorts fed his addiction by supplying him with unlimited amounts of credit. The casino executives knew Dave couldn't sustain those kinds of losses, but still believed Resorts would be made whole when he eventually crashed and burned.

I believe that all this humiliation could end up producing something good for others suffering from gambling addictions. But it's agonizing for all the family. Articles about the Resorts suit begin appearing the day after it's filed. The Philadelphia Inquirer carries a story headlined, "Builder, woman, suspected of $4.7 million casino fraud." The front page of Atlantic City's The Press, bears the headline, "Resorts, Developer Trade Suits Over Dice Debts."

We're all deeply hurt by the public shaming Dave endures in the media. Louise takes it especially hard. She is embarrassed that the entire world now knows about Dave's gambling and about his relationship with another woman. Every lurid detail of the accusations against him appear in the pages of the papers. Even worse, she now must confront the truth that she has ignored or dismissed all of this time: that Dave is having an affair with Martha. Normally she relishes time spent with her wide circle of friends, but Louise now rarely ventures out except to do errands and grocery shopping. She stops volunteering and even skips her weekly bridge games. The isolation only compounds her sense of powerlessness and resentment.

Dave notices Louise's wan face and the circles under her eyes. Guilt overwhelms his pride, and he offers a deeply felt apology, one that isn't encumbered by self-justification and rationalizations.

"Louise, I am so sorry for how much I have hurt you. I clearly lost control over my gambling, but that's no excuse. I take responsibility for what I've done."

He takes her gently by the shoulders and looks into her eyes.

"I am and will forever be grateful to you for sticking by me. I don't know if you can ever forgive me. I wouldn't blame you if you want to leave me."

Louise pulls away, and drops her face in her hands.

"Dave, If I was going to leave you, I should have done it a long time ago," she replies. "What you're putting us all through is inexcusable, gambling illness or no. I don't know if I can ever forgive you. But now is not the time for me to leave. Now, we need to keep our family together. We have to survive this."

Martha's reaction to the lawsuit couldn't be more different. She is apoplectic and can't stop yelling at Dave on the phone.

"'Resorts is just bluffing', you said," she screams at him, throwing his own words back in his face.

"'I have it all under control', you said. 'I'll take full responsibility for your debt and pay them back', you said." Martha pauses for breath.

"Dave, I released my security to you because you were going to make this go away. How could your judgment be so wrong? My reputation is destroyed."

She then raises the issue of money yet again. "You owe me $3 million. I want that money now," she demands. "Since you're no longer settling with Resorts, that's what you need to do. And I want my security interest back. That is what we agreed to if you didn't settle."

Dave's stomach turns into the old, familiar, painful knots. He hangs up.

Soon after the lawsuits become public, the New Jersey Housing Finance Agency and HUD, the federal housing agency, temporarily suspend all government financing for any projects in which Dave has a financial interest, until they can review his business dealings. At the same time, the Division of Gaming Enforcement publicly announces that it is launching its own investigation into the credit dispute between Dave and Resorts. What Dave has feared so much has become a reality: His reputation is in tatters and his career as a housing developer stops dead in its tracks. His West Coast partners halt any further financing of his projects. In addition, he must relinquish all of his ownership interest in several government-financed projects so the projects can close. It's déjà vu for Dave: Once again, the consequences of his compulsive gambling has forced him to sell his interest in several projects at a big loss.

As he struggles to come to grips with what has happened, and accept that he was gambling compulsively,

Dave reaches out to Arnie Wexler, the executive director of the National Council on Compulsive Gambling in New Jersey. Arnie is a well-known figure among those who are fighting for authorities to recognize gambling addiction as a disease. He's a former compulsive gambler himself, and frequently comments in the press. Arnie talks Dave into attending Gamblers Anonymous, and arranges to meet Dave at his first meeting. Dave asks me to accompany them.

"I don't want to go alone. It will make it easier to take this step if you join me," he says.

I don't think either of us recognizes the irony of my joining him now, just as I had tagged along on his gambling outings in the old days.

We attend a Thursday night meeting at a Presbyterian church in Perth Amboy, N.J., about 30 minutes from Elizabeth. The meeting takes place in a drab windowless basement with bare, gray walls. Arnie, his freckled face bearing a welcoming smile, greets Dave as we enter the meeting room. About 15 people sit on folding chairs around a long thin table. There's only one woman in the group. A table with coffee and cookies stands against one of the walls. Dave fills out the sign-in sheet, following other attendees' lead by scribbling down his name as "Dave Z" and his phone number in Elizabeth. Everyone who shows up will get a copy of the list; they can call each other if they need help or just to talk. Everyone introduces themselves (using only their first names) and a few tell the group a short story about how they ended up in this bunker-like room. It's clear that compulsive gamblers liken themselves to alcoholics. In fact, the 12-step program for gamblers is closely modeled on that of Alcoholics Anonymous. Both groups believe the only way to break their compulsion is by complete abstinence.

Seated next to Dave is a tall thin man, in his mid-30s but already slightly balding. Rising from his chair, he confides that because of his gambling, he can't pay his mortgage; he's about to lose his house. He has a wife and two young children. Then he describes gambling's terrible grip on him. He had hidden $14,000 in cash in the trunk of his car, and he couldn't resist heading off to the casino with the cash, in spite of all his existing problems. Just one win would fix everything, he told himself. Of course, he lost all that money. As he tells his story, his face reflects enormous guilt and pain. He loves his family, he says, but he's so addicted that gambling comes before anything else. To Dave, this sounds sadly familiar.

Around the table, others nod with recognition and empathy. When it's Dave Z's turn to speak, he stands up slowly and looks around the table without meeting anyone's eyes. The shame on his face, and the way his shoulders slump, devastate me. I've never seen my father so dejected and humbled. My hands are clammy as he begins to speak.

"My name is Dave," he starts, then pauses to swallow as he clasps his fists together to keep them from shaking. "I thought I could control my gambling. I was wrong. I lost everything. I almost lost my family. Thank you." He sits down, his forehead glistening with sweat.

After the meeting, Arnie gives Dave the names of several psychiatrists who specialize in compulsive gambling. When Dave stiffens at the mention of a psychiatrist, Arnie puts his hand on his shoulder.

"Look Dave, you have a serious illness. If you were having a heart attack you wouldn't hesitate to see a cardiologist. This is no different."

I find myself nodding to Dave to reinforce Arnie's recommendation.

"I've never needed a shrink in my life," Dave protests tentatively. But he takes the cards that Arnie is extending to him with a pained look on his face.

"Trust me, this is a critical part of your recovery," Arnie says quietly. "You can't afford to skip it. Don't hesitate to give me a call anytime if you need to talk. Mutual support is another key part of our group."

The men shake hands and Arnie leaves Dave standing at the table, staring doubtfully at the business cards in his hand.

CHAPTER 9: ON THE HOT SEAT

By now Dave's given up any hope of resolving things easily and rapidly. In January 1981, the New Jersey Division of Criminal Justice opens a criminal investigation into Dave's activities. It empanels a grand jury to gather evidence, hear testimony and ultimately to determine how Dave obtained an unprecedented amount of credit and whether any of this money was taken from the casino for Dave's personal use or as part of a skimming operation. The criminal investigation is led by Steve Secare, the Deputy Attorney General. Secare is a by-the-book prosecutor but fairly affable in one-on-one interactions. Goldstein continues to play hardball and refuses to let Dave cooperate in any way with the investigation. He expects that there will be an indictment and criminal trial; that the best defense for Dave is not to cooperate. The grand jury interviews many Resorts personnel, New Jersey detectives who had investigated the matter, and the investigators of the Division of Gaming Enforcement.

Martha is lying low in Montreal, but the investigation soon catches up with her. She receives a call from the Royal Canadian Mounted Police, who want to talk with her about her relationship with Dave. They tell her they're investigating the criminal charges at the request of the New Jersey Division of Criminal Justice. A Sergeant Gore, tall, heavyset, and gruff looking, shows up with his partner at Martha's apartment. They spend the day reviewing her financial records. She agrees to write to her banks, authorizing them to discuss her affairs with Gore.

Increasingly worried that she, too, is under investigation, Martha decides to call Steve Secare, whose name she had obtained from Gore. She arranges to meet with him the following week. Dave begs her not to talk with Secare or at least to go with an attorney if she does. He offers to pay for the attorney. But she stubbornly refuses.

She takes a bus from Montreal to Trenton to meet with Secare; it's a 12-hour trip. As the bus bumps and rattles over the highway, Martha shifts uncomfortably on the flattened cushion of her seat, and avoids touching the grimy arm rests. It's almost like a dream now: the days when expenses were Dave's responsibility and she flew first class. But she's undertaking this trip on her own initiative and her own dime. Sighing, Martha grits her teeth and stares out the window at the passing countryside.

At the meeting, Secare and another Deputy Attorney General working on the Zarin case assure her that she isn't the target of the criminal investigation and grab the chance to ask her in person for more details about her relationship with Dave. She cooperates fully, while also insisting that Dave is an honorable man who never did anything improper, and certainly nothing illegal.

Despite Martha's spirited defense of Dave in her conversations with the prosecutors, when she talks to him herself, she continues to nag him about money. Where is the $3 million that he owes her? What about her security interest in Dave's assets?

In February, Dave gets a call from Gerry Pollack, Martha's brother. Gerry and his wife had visited Dave and

Martha several times at Resorts as Dave's comped guests and they had become friends with Dave. Now, Gerry invites Dave and Martha to his apartment in Miami, Florida, in the hope of brokering some kind of truce between them. This is the first time in months that Dave and Martha have seen each other or spent time together.

The evening after they arrive in Florida, Gerry, Dave and Martha are having a friendly drink on Gerry's balcony overlooking Biscayne Bay. Gerry opens the discussion.

"Dave, Martha tells me she advanced you a lot of money when you were both at Resorts," he says, in a calm and non-confrontational manner. "Much of it was critical to your business operations. She tells me that in the last nine-month period, she provided you with over $3 million."

Dave shifts in his chair, carefully masking his irritation.

"This money is still owed to her," Gerry continues keeping his tone friendly and choosing his words carefully. "She's anxious about getting this back. She's not just worried about herself but she's also concerned that her son will always have the money to take care of himself in the future."

Gerry pauses and glances at Martha. "I'm not sure I understand the reason for your disagreement," he adds, quietly. "It saddens us to see you arguing over this. Dave, we'd hate for this to come between you two."

Dave ignores Gerry's insinuation that he and Martha have a future as a couple. When he responds, his voice holds a note of frustration.

"Look Gerry, Martha has been a great friend to me and has at times – without my asking – loaned me money, which was critical to my business," Dave says. "And I'll never forget that. She also advanced me lots of money to gamble with, at my urging. More importantly, she has stood by me through all of the difficulties I am going through now. I can never thank her enough for that."

Martha interjects, going straight to her main bone of contention.

"I want my security back, which I released on the condition Dave settles with Resorts," she says, her voice growing harsher. "He didn't come through, though, and now we are in this terrible predicament."

Dave turns to look at Martha.

"I do owe you money," he tells her, calmly. "And I'll pay you back as soon as I can." Dave looks back at Gerry.

"But I don't owe her that kind of money," he declares. "I'm taking full responsibility for and will pay her debt to Resorts, a total of $1.2 million. Martha stopped payment on these checks, so money never left her account." Dave pauses.

"I also gave her over $2 million in certified checks to cover the checks she wrote to Resorts on my behalf. But she never returned those checks to me."

Dave spells out the details of the impact his gambling addiction had on him during that crucial period.

"I had no idea how many cashier's checks I was writing for Martha to take to Canada. I was too absorbed in my gambling to pay attention," he explains. "In my frenzied mood, I didn't notice that I wasn't getting my checks back."

As he recounts his saga yet again, Dave's voice rises in anger.

"But now the accounting has been done on that. So it's simply not true that I owe her $3 million."

Gerry gives everyone a few moments to calm down.

"So what do you think you owe her, Dave?" he eventually asks.

"I don't know, precisely" Dave replies. "But it can't be more than $1 million."

The discussion goes on for a long time. As it does, Martha becomes increasingly strident and Dave grows more tense and irritable. Gerry finally interjects, holding up his hands to halt the bickering.

"Can we agree on the amount of $1 million as the debt Dave owes? That seems like a fair number," he says. Turning to Dave, Gerry asks, "would that be acceptable to you?"

"Yes, I can agree to that amount," replies Dave.

"And you, Martha?" Gerry asks, looking at her beseechingly.

"I'll agree to that figure only if I can get security on Dave's assets to ensure I will get paid," she replies.

Gerry looks at Dave. "That seems fair to me, Dave. What about it?"

"I can't do that, and Martha knows it," Dave retorts, infuriated.

"I'll need to assign my assets to Resorts to get a settlement. And that's a settlement for *both* of us, I might add. Resolving this matter with them has to be the priority right now."

Gerry pauses and looks at Martha's scowling face.

"I can't believe we're having this conversation," Gerry says regretfully. "I want both of you to work this matter out."

Martha fixes her eyes on Dave as he shifts in his seat and avoids making eye contact with either of them.

"Like I said, Gerry, Martha has been a great friend to me and I'm going to pay Martha back," Dave says. "She knows I've always been honest with her."

Martha's eyes narrow; her mouth is pressed into a straight line. Gerry says nothing as he turns toward the balcony railing and watches a speedboat roar past the condo complex toward the ocean.

Over the rest of the weekend, Martha tries several times to hash out the issue of the security agreement, but they can't resolve anything. Dave heads back to Louise in Elizabeth, and Martha flies back to her son in Montreal.

***

Meanwhile, Jon is meeting regularly with Goldstein and Raymar to discuss their aggressive strategy in both the criminal investigation and the Resorts civil suit. In one of these meetings, Goldstein tells Jon that the prosecutors handling Dave's case want to talk with him.

"They may want to investigate your involvement with Dave in this scheme," Goldstein tells him. Jon is stunned, and incensed by Goldstein's choice of words.

"What scheme are you talking about? There's no 'scheme'."

Goldstein doesn't bat an eye,

"It's just that I need to be clear and upfront. If they're investigating you now, Jon, then Dave and I won't be able to have any more attorney-client privileged conversations with you."

Now Jon is seething. "You're trying to stop me from talking to my client on this case. That's outrageous."

A few days later Jon receives a subpoena requiring him to testify before the grand jury in Trenton. He appears before the panel, whose members lob questions at him for about half an hour, most of them about the $80,000 cash deposit he made at Dave's request at the Guarantee Bank. Jon is drained when he leaves the grand jury room, as Steve Secare approaches him. "Can I talk to you?" he asks. Jon nods wearily and Secare ushers him into a small, empty office and closes the door.

Secare gets to the point. "How come Goldstein wouldn't let us talk to you?"

Jon is startled by Secare's question; his eyes widen in surprise. "What are you talking about?"

Secare shrugs; he's as baffled as Jon is.

"Goldstein told us you wouldn't talk to us," he tells Jon. "It made us suspicious about you, about what was going on."

Jon is incredulous. "Goldstein never told me you wanted to talk with me. There's no reason in the world that he should have said that to you. Of course, I would have met with you."

Secare locks eyes with Jon's and remains silent. But his look suggests volumes to Jon: Goldstein isn't serving his client well. Jon understands the message clearly:

Goldstein's hardline approach with investigators, his refusal to allow Dave to cooperate at all, and now, this failure to let Jon communicate with Secare, is not helping Dave.

Jon leaves Trenton still incredulous at what Secare has told him about Goldstein's behavior. While he considers the possibility that Secare is trying to manipulate him, his gut tells him that Secare isn't the type to play games. By the time he meets Dave in his office in Elizabeth, Jon is convinced that Goldstein needs to be replaced. After Jon tells Dave about his conversation with Secare, both agree it's time to find a new lawyer.

Dave calls his brother, Ira, for advice. One of Ira's colleagues recommends that Dave talk to Dino Bliablias, a 52-year-old former prosecutor in Essex County, N.J. Dino is now a partner in a small law firm also based in Newark. Dino's disarming, soft-spoken manner reassures even the most jittery of his clients. His rumpled suit and tousled brown hair remind me of the disheveled 1970s television detective Columbo, famous for always wearing a baggy trench coat. Like Columbo, Dino comes off as a bit confused and disorganized, while all the time noticing and remembering even the smallest detail. Without fanfare, Columbo methodically pieces the clues together, and solves the case. We hope that Dino will work a similar miracle for Dave.

The first step is for Dino to decide whether to let Dave testify before a grand jury. Like any experienced criminal attorney, Dino never lets his clients testify. This time, after spending several hours discussing the case with both Dave and the prosecutors, Dino considers making a rare exception. He's convinced that Dave is going to be indicted, no matter what he does or what he says. His testimony won't change the arc of the case. After all, it will be tough for the jurors, the prosecutors and even average people to believe there wasn't anything illegal going on. How else could someone get so much credit and then take out so much cash from the casino? They'll conclude that there had to be something nefarious going on. The concept of compulsive gambling and the casino as an enabler is new to them. After all, Resorts is the first casino to operate in New Jersey.

Dino wants Dave to help both the prosecutors and the grand jury understand just how this *could* and did happen, and to place Dave's compulsion to gamble front and center. Dino is convinced that Dave is astute and articulate enough to do this. Still, it's a very risky move on Dino's part and one that most other criminal defense lawyers would criticize as reckless.

But first Dino must determine the effectiveness of using a gambling addiction as a defense strategy. So he arranges for Dave to meet with Robert T. Latimer, a recognized psychiatrist in this nascent field of compulsive gambling. (Latimer had been one of the individuals Arnie Wexler had recommended Dave meet with.) Having never visited a psychiatrist before, Dave doesn't know what to expect when he arrives at Dr. Latimer's suburban New Jersey office.

To his surprise, the office isn't in a medical building but at the rear of an old Victorian house. Dave walks through the backyard and opens the door to find a small waiting room. As Dave enters, Dr. Latimer, a tall lanky man in his late 50s, emerges from his office, greets him, and escorts him into the inner office. It's a modest, tidy space, and the doctor directs Dave to settle down comfortably onto a beige sofa against one wall. Dave looks out windows that line one wall of the room. The view fills him with hope: In the middle of the yard stands a large, stately oak tree, studded with the first green shoots of spring.

Dr. Latimer sits down in a well-worn armchair across from Dave. He asks Dave to explain why he is there for this consultation. Dave explains it's actually his attorney's suggestion.

"I'm in a lot of legal and financial trouble because of my excessive gambling at Resorts in Atlantic City," he tells the psychiatrist. "Dino, my attorney, tells me I'm about to be criminally indicted for it." Dave catches himself tapping his fingers on the sofa cushion and stops.

"Well," Dr. Latimer says, "why don't you tell me how this came about?"

Dave hesitates. "That could take a long time."

"Don't worry," Dr. Latimer says "I blocked out the entire afternoon for our meeting. Take all the time you need."

Dave launches into the story, the one he first told us many months ago and has recounted again and again since.

Dr. Latimer asks Dave about his childhood and takes careful notes. Dave describes his family, and his college years. He describes his first experience of gambling when he worked at the Navy Yard in Philadelphia.

"It helped with my boredom. And it was exciting," he says.

Dave describes his work habits: He's compulsive about his business and sometimes works around the clock until people tell him to snap out of it. He acknowledges that he is a workaholic.

He tells Dr. Latimer that he's suffering from insomnia; his legal, personal and financial problems are making him anxious, moody and depressed. He thinks almost obsessively about his legal difficulties and what he's putting his family through.

Dr. Latimer asks Dave about Louise.

"She wants very little; she hates the publicity. She's so embarrassed that she won't see people," Dave says.

"Even going to the supermarket has become traumatic for her. Once, recently, she abandoned her full shopping cart just to avoid having to talk to a neighbor in the checkout line ahead of her." Dave pauses.

"I've put her through so much over the years, I feel incredibly guilty."

Dave's eyes fill with tears and he takes several minutes to pull himself together. Dr. Latimer hands Dave a box of tissues, but otherwise doesn't try to comfort him or break his train of thought. Once Dave recovers, he looks up at Dr. Latimer.

"I can't believe she's sticking by me. She's keeping our family together. I'm so grateful. I owe her everything."

Then Dr. Latimer starts to dig more deeply.

"You mentioned this person, Martha Nemtin. Tell me about her."

Dave gives the psychiatrist a short version of how their affair started, then offers a self-analysis. "I think Martha represented another level of excitement for me. I justified my attraction by telling myself that I needed someone who could understand my business, the stresses I was going through. But I now realize that I was wrong. Martha reinforced the worst in me."

His voice is wavering; he begins to weep again and reaches out blindly for the box of tissues.

"What I really need is what I've had all along – a warm, loving person, who will support me through thick and thin and do everything to keep our family together. Louise has always known this. I guess I'm learning it now, the hard way; and she's paying the price."

Dave provides more details about his affair, partnership and financial dependence on Martha, and how their relationship is devolving into constant arguing over money.

Dr. Latimer brings the conversation back to his gambling at Resorts, particularly during the four-month period that ended in April of 1980.

"What was on your mind when this was happening?" Dr. Latimer asks.

Dave reflects for a minute, takes a deep breath and slowly exhales.

"I went wild. I had no idea what I was doing or what I was losing. I couldn't stop," he says.

"But what were you thinking, Dave?" Dr. Latimer probes. "What was going on inside of you at this time – when you were gambling 16 hours each day for 40 to 50 days at a time, what was crossing your mind?"

"I was completely immersed in it. It was like a drug."

Dave then repeats what he's once told Martha: "It's better than sex." He stands up and starts to pace up and down the room as he recalls the sensations.

"The pleasure was so intense that I thought of nothing else. I couldn't think about business, my family, my health

– nothing. While it was going on I wasn't thinking, I just had to keep gambling. Like a machine."

Dave pauses and sits down. He's feeling over-exposed and vulnerable. He's never really taken such a deep look into his soul, much less revealed so much of himself to another person. Dave looks directly at Dr. Latimer.

"The pain, the shame, the suffering of my family has been horrible," he adds, quietly. "My reputation, my whole life is in shambles. When you're out of control, how do you gain control? I had never realized that I was a compulsive gambler until I went to Gamblers Anonymous. I heard horror stories there."

The meeting with the psychiatrist helps Dave articulate his physical and emotional state while he was gambling and to summon the courage to discuss these emotions publicly. On April 23, 1981, almost a year to the day of his confession to Jon, Rich and me in the Sinatra suite, Dave appears before the grand jury and testifies for five hours. He explains his entire gambling history, in painful detail. He spells out just how he covered these losses from his own funds or by borrowing from banks and individuals and business partners, often secured by future earnings from his projects. He describes how Resorts' de facto limitless credit spurred him to rack up astronomic debt to the casino. Meanwhile, casino executives had repeatedly asked to invest in his development projects so that Resorts could get credit for making investments in affordable housing.

On May 7, 1981, Dave is indicted on 93 counts of theft by deception. Each of the 82 checks he wrote to Resorts and that banks later returned for insufficient funds represent a single count; the eleven markers Dave signed at the Boardwalk Regency make up the remaining 11 counts. Each count carries a maximum penalty of five years in prison. The indictment hits Dave like a thunderbolt. Dino had warned him that an indictment was unavoidable, but, ever the optimist, Dave still had hoped that his testimony would persuade the prosecutors and grand jury that he never had any criminal intent or did anything illegal.

Meanwhile, the newspapers describe the charges in unsparing, sometimes sensational detail. The Philadelphia Inquirer informs the world in bold print: "Developer indicted in casino credit swindle."

The headline on the front page of The Press: "Developer Charged with $4.3M. Casino Credit Fraud."

Dave hasn't warned Louise about the upcoming indictment, as he doesn't want to worry her. His decision backfires; an avalanche of negative newspaper articles blindsides her. Once again, she feels embarrassed and ashamed. This soft-spoken woman, who hates confrontation, now is white with rage.

"How could you do this to me, to all of us?" she yells at Dave, totally distraught. Then, once again, she shuts herself in their bedroom.

CHAPTER 10: ROAD TO RECOVERY

Several days after Dave's criminal indictment, the Division of Gaming Enforcement files a civil complaint with the Casino Control Commission charging Resorts and six employees, including Gary Grant, Gary Thompson, Bill Gallion and Randy Mhelic, with numerous credit violations of the New Jersey Casino Control Act regarding their handling of Dave's gambling activities. Alleging that the manner in which Resorts extended credit to Dave violates the law, the division asks that Resorts' gambling license be suspended, and for the casino and several of its executives to be hit with hefty fines. The complaint states that Resorts' conduct raises serious questions regarding its financial integrity and responsibility. The Atlantic City Press headline reads, "6 Resorts Employees Charged." James Zazzali, the New Jersey attorney general, tells *The Press* that Resorts is to blame for irresponsibly advancing funds to a compulsive gambler and for failing to adhere to the State's casino credit restrictions.

The following week Dino arranges for Dave to meet with another psychiatrist recommended by Arnie Wexler. Dr. Robert L. Custer, the world's foremost expert on compulsive gambling, is a psychiatrist at the Veterans Administration headquarters and will provide Dave's legal team with a second opinion. In 1974, Dr. Custer founded the National Foundation for the Study and Treatment of Pathological Gambling. "We're dealing with a behavior disorder," Dr.

Custer declared when the group opened its doors. Largely thanks to his efforts, the American Psychiatric Association formally classified compulsive gambling as a psychological disorder in 1980.

Dave meets with Dr. Custer in the latter's home in Bethesda, Maryland. At six feet, with a football player's build, the balding 53-year-old physician cuts an imposing figure. Dave meets with him twice, with each meeting lasting about four hours. Their discussions follow similar lines to Dave's visit with Dr. Latimer. Dr. Custer explores Dave's lack of judgment and self-control. He also explains to Dave that gambling addiction is only now beginning to be acknowledged as an illness by the medical community and that the public remains largely unaware of it.

With the family in turmoil, I take a four-month leave of absence from my job in the General Counsel's Office of the U.S. Department of Commerce to assist in Dino's defense of my father. My wife, our three-month-old son, Brian, and I move into my parents' modest two–bedroom apartment in Elizabeth. Living with each other in such close quarters, our presence immediately changes the atmosphere at home. My mother seems rejuvenated by her role as grandmother and once again busies herself preparing elaborate dinners for a table full of people.

Although Dave is terrified by the prospect of going to prison, having his grandson to coddle lifts his spirits and the baby's coos and gurgles lighten everyone's mood. Rich and Susan come over often for dinner with their two young daughters and newborn son. Robin joins us from Chicago when she can. My siblings and all our spouses are determined to support our parents and help extricate Dave from the mess he created for himself. Dave is just as determined to change his life and becomes deeply committed to Gamblers Anonymous; he attends the meetings weekly. We have no time for recriminations; instead, we're intent on piecing our family back together amidst the turmoil.

Although she hides it, it's toughest for Louise to get over her anger. Who can blame her? Many of Louise's friends abandon her and she's deeply hurt by this. When she does venture out, she's afraid of bumping into gossipy acquaintances asking rude and painful questions.

Once at the pharmacy, she runs into a woman she barely knows. "I'm so sorry to hear about Dave's situation in the papers," the woman says to her with undisguised smugness in her voice. "We all feel for you, Louise. You must be livid."

Other customers near them stop and stare. Louise backs away, the blood rushing to her face. Angry and embarrassed, she flees the pharmacy without her medications. One of us later returns to pick them up for her.

Dave gets more bad news in June when the Department of Housing and Urban Development and the New Jersey financial agencies formally block Dave and all of his affiliated companies from participating in any projects involving government funds. Now that he's blacklisted by HUD, Dave must relinquish ownership and control in all of his projects in the pipeline or under development in New Jersey and Pennsylvania. He's forced to sell his stakes in all of his partnerships at a considerable loss, yet still owes his partners the money they advanced to him for all the projects that now are suspended. Dave goes into his office in Elizabeth every day, but there is not much for him to do other than to unwind various projects. Only Nina, his secretary, continues to work for him. To save the management company he owns jointly with Rich, he transfers all of his interest in the company to my brother. It is a total personal and financial disaster for him.

Every day I go to Dino's law firm to develop Dave's defense strategy as part of a small team of lawyers that include Dino, his partner Ken McGuire, and Jon. At one of these sessions Jon says to Dino, "I have been reading about the Pre-Trial Intervention Program in New Jersey for first-time offenders. Would Dave be eligible for this?"

Dino raises his eyebrows.

"PTI is designed for first-time offenders – typically charged with a non-violent crime – to enter a rehabilitation program instead of going to trial," he says, turning to me to explain what Jon is talking about. "The program usually includes required community service and restitution. Someone who successfully completes the program, can have criminal charges dismissed and their record expunged."

Dino pauses, looks up to the ceiling for a moment. "But this program, so far, only has been used for minor offenses, such as possession of a small quantity of drugs, burglary or shoplifting. It's a stretch for the program to admit a wealthy gambler, charged with fraud of substantial amounts of money."

Still, Dino is willing to give it a shot. "Let me do some research."

A week later, Dino comes back with encouraging news.

"Jon, I like your idea of trying to get Dave accepted into the PTI program. Actually, in many ways, he's the perfect candidate." Not only did Dave have no prior record, Dino argues that since he had no criminal intent, it's not likely the state will convict him on the criminal charges. "It's clear he could be rehabilitated. But—" Dino stops, and a serious expression crosses his face. "It'll be tough to convince the criminal division to apply the PTI statute in such a high-profile case. It's a real long shot."

Even if the odds aren't great, I tell Dino that we should try. "What would be the first step?" I ask him. "What would we need to do?"

Dino gives me a tight smile. "I'll meet with Zazzali, the attorney general. We used to work together."

James Zazzali is 43 years old, tall, thin, with an engaging smile. He greets Dino warmly in his large office in Trenton. After reminiscing about their time together in the prosecutor's office, Jim looks at his watch. "Dino, I just fit you in because you said it was important," he says, cutting to the chase. "What do you want to discuss?"

Dino gives a quick summary of Dave's case and makes a pitch for Pre-Trial Intervention. When he finishes, Jim smiles.

"You're going to have to do better than that," he says. "I know a little about this case, mostly about the charges against Resorts. Zarin's story is interesting. But come on, Dino, do you really expect me to believe Zarin could have gambled that much, or taken that much money out of the casino, without a clear fraudulent plan? Besides, I'm told he went all the way to Canada to open a bank account. That seems to me like a pretty clear intent to defraud."

Disappointed, Dino shakes Zazzali's hand. "Well, thanks for hearing me out, Jim."

The next day Dino's in a foul mood and tells us how unlikely it will be to change Zazzali's mind. "Even so, I'm not giving up on this, though," he adds. "Not yet."

He then asks me to review all of the grand jury testimony. "I want you to prepare a brief that will go to Zazzali, Secare, the lead prosecutor, and Stephen Imperiale, the director of the Pre-Trial Intervention program. We'll need to show, first, just how weak the prosecutor's case is."

Dino's voice rises. "And we need to make a compelling case for why a high-profile gambler, one who has accomplished so much good in developing housing for seniors and the underprivileged, is exactly the kind of person intended for this program."

Dino tells me he'll need the brief within the next week, and I set to work on it immediately.

It's clear to me, after reviewing the grand jury testimony, that Dave probably wouldn't be convicted in a criminal trial. He didn't deceive Resorts casino; its officials knew everything Dave was doing. Indeed, they were his enablers. Resorts management, particularly Gary Grant, made it clear to the grand jury that everyone knew, in Grant's words, that Dave "could not continuously produce this kind of money." Knowing that, Resorts continued to extend him unlimited credit because it believed Dave's projects generated enough profit that it would recoup its money. I used Dave's testimony and that of the Resorts executives to the grand jury as the foundation for my brief to Zazzali and Stephen Imperiale, the director of PTI.

Dino sends a detailed letter and my supporting brief to Zazzali, Secare and Imperiale on June 4, 1981. The letter states that the "interests of the State of New Jersey will best be served by permitting Mr. Zarin to participate in the Pre-Trial Intervention Program." Dino encloses the psychiatric evaluations of Dr. Robert T. Latimer and Dr. Robert L. Custer.

**

By now Dave and Martha's relationship is progressing from cool to icy. Almost every phone conversation they have centers on Martha's constant demand for the $3 million she insists he owes her, together with the return of her security. Still, Dave retains some sense of loyalty to Martha, and it's important to him to resolve these financial issues. So when she arrives in New York to visit relatives in New Hope, Pennsylvania, Dave picks her up from the Drake Hotel in Manhattan to drive her there. Emerging from the hotel lobby, Martha greets Dave with a broad smile and hug. However, as soon as she settles into the seat next to Dave, she launches into her familiar refrain: a demand for the money. "Dave, you can't keep avoiding your obligations."

"Martha, for God's sake, give it a rest."

Dave is gripping the steering wheel so tightly that his knuckles are turning white. Their squabble grows louder and more bitter as they leave Manhattan and enter New Jersey.

"If it weren't for you, this horror show would never have happened!" Dave exclaims in fury. "I never told this to the grand jury, or the prosecutors, or to your brother Gerry. But I am telling you now. You're as much a cause of this as I am. And for you to demand this kind of money when I don't owe it to you is outrageous."

Martha explodes. "How dare you try to put the blame on me, after all I have done for you! You can't use that argument to get out of paying me the money you owe."

Dave spots the highway exit for Hoboken and steers into the off ramp. As he drives to the town center Martha is confused. She's finally silent. Dave pulls up alongside a taxi stand, stops the car, and gets out. He opens the trunk, yanks out Martha's bag and marches over to the first taxi driver idling in line.

"How much do you charge to drive to New Hope?" Dave asks him.

The driver looks at him in surprise. "It'll cost you at least $150."

Dave whips out his wallet, pulls out two $100 bills and hands them to the driver.

"Here you go."

He dumps Martha's valise into the trunk of the taxi and beckons her over.

"This guy'll take you to New Hope, Martha. I can't do this anymore."

In shock, Martha climbs into the back seat of the cab. For the first time since Dave picked her up, she's speechless.

"Goodbye, Martha."

Dave slams her door shut, and waves at the driver. Dave stares after the cab, exhausted but relieved.

***

As attempts to win approval for Dave's acceptance into the PTI program move forward, we know that he'll need to make restitution. And, even if the case does end up going to trial, it will be important for Dave's criminal defense to show he has reimbursed the casinos the money he owed them. Dino determines that it will be easiest to hammer out the first settlement with Boardwalk Regency Hotel, to which Dave owes the smallest sums. After getting Dave's agreement, Dino directs Jon to contact the general counsel of Caesars and begin settlement discussions. On July 22, 1981, Dave and Caesars reach a settlement for full payment. At Dave's request, payments would be first applied to Martha's $205,000 debt to Caesars, then to Dave's $250,000 outstanding debt to Caesars. Installments would be payable annually over four years.

In early August, Dino speaks on the phone with Stephen Imperiale, who is non-committal, but says he'd like to meet with Dave. Dave returns to Atlantic City to meet with the him. The PTI office, located on the first floor of a five-story office building on Atlantic Avenue, has only four employees and a small budget. Imperiale, a tall man with a stocky build and a military crew cut has a no-nonsense manner. He ushers Dave into his office, a small room with a window overlooking an alley, and furnished only with a small desk and some chairs. Dave shakes hands with Imperiale and settles into the chair in front of his desk. Imperiale skips the small talk.

"Mr. Zarin, you're a very unusual candidate for us to consider for admission into the program. We've never considered anyone charged with 93 separate counts of fraud, involving millions of dollars. So you have a high threshold to overcome."

Dave nods in understanding. "I appreciate the opportunity to talk with you."

Imperiale then asks Dave a series of questions about the extent of his gambling, his indebtedness, his cycling of cash and his decision to open two bank accounts in Canada– and whether the casino was aware of it. Dave answers each question in painstaking detail; he emphasizes that he informed casino executives personally about what he was doing and why.

"I had only one overriding goal, an obsession: to keep gambling," he explains. "So I needed to be sure that all of the checks I was writing to Resorts to pay my gambling debts cleared."

"Now," Dave adds, "I fully intend to repay that money."

Imperiale pauses for a moment, then asks a crucial question. Mr. Zarin, are you still gambling?"

"No, I am not," Dave says forcefully. "I have been attending Gamblers Anonymous weekly for the past eight months. It has been eye-opening. I never realized it before, but now I know I have an illness."

"But isn't this illness similar to alcoholism?" Imperiale presses. "One drink, and you resume your old behavior?"

"Quite honestly, I don't believe that I'll ever gamble again," Dave says. His addiction, he explains, destroyed his life's work and his reputation as a savvy and responsible developer.

"I've nearly lost my wife and family. The prospect of going to jail frightens me so much that whenever I think about gambling, I feel sick to my stomach," Dave confesses.

The next day, Dino talks over the phone with Imperiale, trying to get a read on how the meeting went. Still non-committal, Imperiale tells Dino that Zarin would need to resolve his debt to Resorts before being considered for admission to PTI.

In late August, 1982, after talking with Dave, Dino calls Joel Sterns, counsel for Resorts.

"Joel, I think it's time that Zarin and Resorts resolve this matter. This stalemate is hurting everyone," says Dino.

Joel agrees to meet for lunch at Lorenzo's, a popular steakhouse in Trenton. The settlement negotiations are a lot simpler this time. Dave is now broke. His liabilities far exceed his assets. He's divested himself of ownership and control in all of his projects under development that require government financing. True, he has some monies still due to him over the next several years from his completed projects. But some of these sums are already pledged to banks.

Resorts is also very anxious to settle. They are facing an admin-istrative hearing over allegations that they violated credit regulations and their casino license is in jeopardy. Nevertheless, Sterns insists, "the settlement can't be a nominal amount. It has to appear meaningful."

Over lunch and several telephone discussions, the framework of a settlement takes final shape. Dave would pay Resorts $250,000 to settle Martha's $1,225,000 debts. He would pay another $500,000 to settle his $3,435,000 debts. He would make installment payments over five years, interest free. All claims and litigations would be terminated. Dave would provide to Resorts, as collateral, the monies still due him and a percentage of his ownership in the Marina Towers partnership. For Dave, it's as good a deal as possible to get out of a bad situation. Most importantly, it also opens the possibility that he could be admitted into the PTI program.

Dave calls Martha to deliver the good news. He excitedly explains that she'll be free of any liability or exposure for the debts; she'll only need to sign a release for Resorts. Martha is silent for a long moment. Then she drops a bombshell.

"Dave, I'm not going to sign a release until you arrange to pay me the $3 million you owe me and provide me with new collateral to replace the collateral I released last year."

Dave is stunned. "Martha, didn't you hear what I just told you?" he demanded. "I just settled all of our debts with Resorts. I'm paying your obligations, as I promised. And we had agreed that I would pay you $1 million, not $3 million. I have no collateral left to give you. I have to give it to Resorts as part of the settlement."

"Well, Dave, I thought about it again," Martha retorts. "You still owe me $3 million. And I want my collateral back."

"That's extortion!" Dave shouts. "I'm not agreeing to that."

Martha hangs up.

When Dino conveys Martha's position to Joel Sterns, Joel is furious.

"You guys are impossible to do a deal with!" he exclaims in outrage. "We can't trust you." The deal is off – again.

After allowing several days to elapse and tempers to cool, Dino restarts negotiations. After all, Resorts has as much to lose as does Dave at this point. Sterns agrees to exclude Martha from the settlement. This time, Dave will pay Resorts $500,000 to settle his debt of $3,435,000. Jon is tasked with drafting the settlement documents with John Donnelly, Stern's law partner.

As a courtesy, Dave calls Martha to tell her he's going forward with the settlement without her, settling only his own debts to Resorts. When Martha begins to yell, Dave hangs up. She is left shouting at a dial tone.

Before Resorts and Dave have a chance to sign their settlement agreement, Martha files a lawsuit against Dave in federal court, alleging that Dave owes her $3 million. In addition, the suit requests a preliminary injunction to stop the settlement between Dave and Resorts.

"An injunction will hurt you very, very badly," Dino warns Dave. "Do you want to settle with Martha? You're not going to get PTI if you don't."

"No way," Dave says, defiantly. "What she's doing is extortion. I want PTI, but I'll go all the way with this thing. No settlement."

Fortunately, Dino and the lawyers for Resorts are able to get the court to deny the request for an injunction, although Martha's civil suit still stands.

On September 28,1981, Dave and Resorts execute the settlement agreement. The *Philadelphia Inquirer* headlines the story in its New Jersey section: "Resorts and $3.43 Million Debtor Settle Suit." After all the drama and brinksmanship during the negotiations, Resorts agrees to accept a modest payment. But it is too late. Both Dave and Resorts have suffered considerable damage to their reputations.

A short while later, Martha files another lawsuit. This time, she's going after Jon, and seeking $5 million in damages, alleging that he conspired to deprive her of valuable property. The allegations rest on Jon's actions when, in his role as Dave's legal advisor, he drew up the documents waiving her security interest in Dave's projects. Martha now claims that Jon helped Dave convince her to act against her best interests by signing the document.

In November 1981, Steve Secare, the prosecutor in Dave's case and the Deputy Attorney General, and PTI Director Stephen Imperiale meet with Jim Zazzali in his office. The subject is Dave's PTI application, which both men are supporting. Zazzali listens to both of them with some disbelief.

"You're telling me that Zarin is really a compulsive gambler and that we should treat it as a real illness?" Zazzali asks.

"More than that," says Secare. "I don't think we could ever get a conviction here. Proving that Zarin defrauded the casino is going to be very difficult." Secare emphasizes the casino's role in the mess.

"They violated a lot of regulations in giving him so much credit," he argues. "They were totally aware of his daily gambling losses and knew they were unsustainable, but still gave him unlimited credit." How, Secare asked, could a jury convict Dave in circumstances like this?

Zazzali turns to Imperiale. "Can Zarin be rehabilitated? Can a compulsive gambler be rehabilitated?"

"His psychiatrists think so," Imperiale answers. "He's convincing when you talk to him, and he's been going to weekly Gamblers Anonymous meetings for almost a year. He's also beginning to do volunteer work with a leading foundation on compulsive gambling and he's settled his debts with every casino."

That said, Imperiale adds that everyone would need to keep a close eye to ensure Dave didn't relapse.

"Okay," says Zazzali, still somewhat skeptical. "Send me your recommendation in writing."

On January 6, 1982, Dave is admitted into the PTI program. Under the terms of the participation agreement, Dave has to report to his PTI counselor monthly for twelve months, continue his participation in Gamblers Anonymous, make restitution of his gambling debts, and perform 100 hours of volunteer community service. Imperiale spells all this out to Dino, who promptly calls Dave with the good news. Dave is euphoric. He has been given a second chance at life. He knows it. He intends to make the most of it. Hearing the news, Louise's body sags in relief, her eyes fill with tears. She has struggled to hold herself and her family together. For the first time in months, she allows herself to think that their ordeal might finally be ending.

A family dinner celebration is in order. All of the kids and grandkids join Dave and Louise for dinner in a private room at Gallaghers steak restaurant in New York. It is a memorable moment for the family. With the worse behind us, we all notice Dave has changed. While he retains his confident and commanding presence, his pride has taken a beating. His hair is much grayer, and he's now a visibly softer more patient man. It's a humbler and more empathetic Dave who gets up to speak to us.

"I am so grateful to every member of this family – including our grandkids," he says, grinning at the toddlers squirming around the table, "for supporting me through this very difficult time. I can't be more sorry. I let all of you down and hurt you all in so many ways. My behavior over the last several years has been inexcusable."

Dave then turns to look directly at Louise. "But I particularly want to apologize to you, Louise. I am very sorry for all the pain I have caused you. I am forever grateful and so lucky that you stood by me and kept our family from falling apart. I don't deserve your love and forgiveness. Not at all."

Dave raises his glass to Louise and says, "I love you all from the bottom of my heart."

CHAPTER 11: BACK IN BUSINESS

Though Dave is a profoundly changed man, he has lost none of his drive and wastes no time in returning to his housing development activities. Once his indictment is dismissed, HUD and the New Jersey HFA will also lift his suspension. Then his business will all go back to normal: He'll once again be able to obtain financing for his projects.

His first step is to call Rafferty.

"I want to you to look for some property that we could get an option on in the South Inlet section," Dave tells him.

Although Dave has spoken to Rafferty in the past about the area, Rafferty is still somewhat skeptical about its potential. The South Inlet neighborhood is Atlantic City's most destitute and dilapidated community. Dave, however, has a vision. He knows that the location abuts both the inlet and the ocean, making it potentially valuable for real estate investors. Where else is it possible to acquire land this cheaply, and have a reasonable chance of making a profit while also transforming the South Inlet into a desirable place to live for middle income residents.

Dave now looks for a new partner to finance his projects. Before his gambling crisis, Dave had met a New York real estate duo who had expressed interest in investing in his housing ventures. Both Richard Friedberg and Roger Greene are unusually colorful characters in the typically buttoned-down world of New York real estate. Friedberg owns a small real estate firm, with an office on Manhattan's Park Avenue and fancies himself as a wheeler-dealer who likes to take risks. The ambitious real estate tycoon, now in his mid-40s, lives in a huge house in Westport, Connecticut and has a chauffeur who drives him around in a gleaming white Rolls Royce. Roger Greene is a tall, thin real estate lawyer, sporting ornately tooled cowboy boots and custom-tailored suits. He gave up his practice to partner with Friedberg on investments.

Dave asks them whether they would be interested in forming a partnership to build affordable housing in Atlantic City. They agree to consider the idea, and Dave offers them a guided tour of his Atlantic City. Meeting up in New York, the three men climb into Friedberg's Rolls Royce and the chauffeur drives them south. Turning on the charm, Dave takes advantage of the long drive with the men to sell them on the tremendous untapped opportunities in the South Inlet.

The duo are very impressed yet hesitant, given Dave's widely publicized gambling scandal.

"What about your gambling, Dave?" asks Roger. "How can we be comfortable that those days are in the past?"

"I've lost all desire to gamble," Dave replies. "I go to Gamblers Anonymous meetings weekly. These days, my focus is finding ways to help compulsive gamblers, not to go back to being one."

Once they reach Atlantic City, they stop to pick up Rafferty who directs the driver to several potential properties in the South Inlet. Before long, Dave knows he's won them over. Together, the three men form a partnership to develop housing in the South Inlet and other sections of Atlantic City. It's a 50-50 deal; Dave has a half interest in the new venture and is the managing partner; Friedberg and Greene split the other half. Dave's new backers agree to fund the operating costs of Dave's office in Elizabeth as well any expenses that will be incurred in Atlantic City. They also agree to provide the guarantees and letters of credit that Dave will need to obtain financing for the South Inlet projects.

Dave is back in business!

His first step is to rehire his entire staff. Then he sets out to buy the plots of land he's been eyeing. Once he has done that, he will finally be able to begin development of Lighthouse Plaza, a 20-story 314-unit middle income rental project in the South Inlet, just north of the boardwalk. Dave envisions it as the catalyst of the transformation of the South Inlet into the jewel of Atlantic City.

Even as Dave looks forward to the rebirth of his business, his personal affairs remain mired in the past. The feud with Martha drags on, with no end in sight. It's bitter and unrelenting, and, to Dave, puzzling. Sure, he understands Martha's concern about getting repaid, but her concern is becoming an obsession and the lawsuit feels like a vendetta. As Martha returns to her hum-drum life in Montreal, she's following Dave's fortunes from afar. How dare he move on with his life? She resents how Dave, newly rehabilitated, survived with his family intact and his business poised to thrive once more. She's not going to let him off the hook.

In late March, Martha again endures a long bus trip from Montreal, this time to Atlantic City to speak with PTI

Director Imperiale. She knows that Imperiale has granted Dave admission to the program, and wants to convince him to put pressure on Dave to pay her what she believes he owes her. Imperiale tells her that he'll raise the matter with Dave, but makes no promises about the outcome.

A frustrated Martha then tries to meet with Judge Porreca, the Superior Court judge overseeing Dave's criminal case and the man who will determine whether or not to dismiss criminal charges. When the judge isn't available, Martha hands his clerk a handwritten letter pleading for his help retrieving the money she insists Dave owes her. Judge Porreca replies to Martha by letter, telling her that if all the parties agree, he'd be happy to meet with everyone involved and see if something can be done. No meeting takes place.

***

Dave's recovery from his troubles is a bumpier process than he'd like, but it's relatively smooth compared to Atlantic City's tortuous path toward economic growth and political stability. The city's chaotic government administration and lingering racial hostilities continue to strangle the City's transformation.

Although Atlantic City has overhauled its governance structure so that voters can directly elect their mayor, the election exacerbates its woes. In July 1982, the two candidates vying to become mayor are Michael Matthews, the commissioner serving as director of Revenue and Finance, and James Usry, the assistant superintendent of public schools. Matthews is white; Usry is a leader in Atlantic City's Black community and the first Black person to run for mayor in the city's history.

There's a stark contrast between the two: the 48-year-old Matthews has a reputation for partying and hanging out with celebrities, while the 6'6"-tall Usry was a former classroom teacher and school principal who once played briefly for the Harlem Globetrotters. The Black community, which makes up about 40 percent of the electorate, comes out in force to support Usry. That turnout helps elect four Black councilmen, but even so, Usry loses the election by a razor thin margin – a mere 359 votes. Alleging irregularities in the absentee vote, Usry refuses to concede the election and challenges the result in court; deepening the chasm between the two groups. The case is dismissed, but nevertheless, on July 1, two separate inaugurations take place. The ceremony for Matthews and five white councilmen takes place in front of City Hall. The ceremony for the four Black councilmen is held in the Old City Commission Chamber, at which Usry gives a defiant keynote speech.

***

Amid the political turmoil in Atlantic City, Dave's legal woes are beginning to fade. On July 14, 1982, the Judge overseeing Dave's criminal case dismisses the indictment against him; then more good news comes the following month: HUD and the New Jersey government agencies notify Dave that they are reinstating him. With the HUD and New Jersey suspensions lifted, Dave is able to participate in HUD and state-financed projects and programs. Dave's record of indictment is expunged from court records several months later.

He moves ahead with getting the Lighthouse Plaza project on the next tax-exempt municipal bond issued by the Atlantic County Improvement Authority.

Ever the astute politician, Dave calls Michael Matthews, the new mayor, to update him on the project, and the anticipated start-up date for construction. Dave knows that after winning a bitter, racially divisive election, Mathews is hungry for positive press. Although he's hospitalized with a back injury, Matthews invites reporters to his hospital room to announce the project as an olive branch to the Black community. It's a public relations coup for both men; and it seals Dave's professional comeback.

Standing at Matthews' bedside, Dave gives the press an upbeat outlook of what still lies ahead for Atlantic City. "Our work here could be the start of a revival in this forgotten part of Atlantic City. Now the time is right for affordable rental units for middle income families."

As Dave resumes his leadership in bringing affordable housing to Atlantic City, he's welcomed back in the fold by the local politicians, civic leaders, and even the local press. As he has so many times in his career, Dave has adroitly turned things around. And yet, there's still one thing he can't control at all: Martha.

Martha continues to feel simmering resentment over all that she sacrificed for him. She loved him, stood by him through so much, even putting him before her own business and financial stability. Now she's being cast off, like an old shoe.

All she wants now is revenge and the money he owes her. When no one calls her to testify in New Jersey's proceedings against Resorts, she takes matters into her own hands. She travels to Trenton and, appearing without counsel, demands the right to speak at the Division of Gaming Enforcement's hearings. The request is an odd one, but the administrative law judge allows it. She seizes the opportunity to once again spell out – in exhausting and exhaustive detail – all her grievances. The judge listens patiently, asks very few questions and remains non-committal. He's not going to weigh in on her side when it comes to her claim against Dave and Resorts. Disappointed, Martha heads back to Montreal and remains even more determined to press her civil suit against Dave.

The next weapon in her arsenal is a third deposition of Dave and they face each other again on September 16, 1982. By this time her lawyer has quit representing her. The proceedings, at Dino's Newark law firm, have an absurd, even surreal, feel. Martha, representing herself, grills Dave on her own, referring to herself throughout in the third person. But many of her questions simply echo those posed in previous depositions. What had Dave said to her; done to her? After a long day of questioning, Dave senses that Martha may be tiring. He sighs to himself with relief; the deposition may be winding down.

Then Martha takes her final jab.

"Mr. Zarin, according to your testimony, you had full rights to that conditional release, the collateral therein," she declares. "Why wasn't Mrs. Nemtin included in the settlement?"

Perplexed, Dave asks, "What settlement?" He can feel his blood pressure spiking.

"The settlement of the action of Resorts versus Zarin and Nemtin," she explains. "You had full rights to the collateral. Why wasn't Mrs. Nemtin included in that settlement?"

"Martha, you're a fraud," Dave says, through clenched teeth.

"Thank you," Martha answers dryly, with a faint smile. "But why wasn't she included –"

"—You're *really* a fraud!"

Martha, for once, doesn't respond to Dave's growing anger. Showing no reaction, she forges on with her question.

"—in view of the fact that Mr. Zarin had full rights to the collateral that was released on May 9, conditionally released, however, but it was released." She pauses, then returns to her main question. "Why was Mrs. Nemtin not included in the settlement?"

"I can't believe what I'm hearing!" Dave says, struggling to control his temper. He pauses to regain his composure.

"But let me answer the question," he finally responds, evenly. "You *were* included in the settlement. You were very much – we settled your case with Resorts only contingent on your signature for a quarter of million dollars. You were *always* included—"

Martha tries to interrupt, but Dave holds up his hand.

"—let me finish. You were always included in this settlement. But you saw fit at the propitious time, what you felt was the propitious time, not to sign the agreement unless I acquiesced to pay you some three million dollars which I refused to do."

Now Dave shows his anger and places both hands flat on the table in front of him.

"To me, it was blackmail of the vilest kind," he says, in an icy tone.

"As a result of you not taking that settlement with Resorts, Resorts vacated the settlement portion with you and we went on, after great effort, after you almost succeeded in destroying the entire settlement, to go on and settle with Resorts. That is the reason we didn't settle for you, Mrs. Nemtin!"

"According to your testimony," Martha states coolly, "since you have the collateral, since it was released, why did you not just finish the settlement including Mrs. Nemtin? Why was it necessary to ask for further releases on the very same document, for the very same collateral, if you already had it?"

Exasperated, Dave runs a hand through his cropped gray curls.

"Mrs. Nemtin, an agreement is with two parties and in this case, it was with three parties. It was with Resorts, with Zarin and Nemtin. We got to the point where Zarin and Resorts agreed but Nemtin didn't agree. When you turned down the settlement, Resorts then refused even to settle with me."

Dave sighs.

"I would ask for a recess for a few minutes," he says, quietly.

"I'm not feeling well and I don't mind if you want to quit," Martha replies.

"That's why I'm asking for a recess. I don't feel well," Dave says, flatly.

They exchange glances across the table. Dave and Martha have exhausted each other.

The next time they meet, it will be in a courtroom.

***

Fresh from the Zarin gambling debacle with Atlantic City's casinos, the New Jersey State Commission of Investigation embarks on an exhaustive inquiry into casino credit policies. The SCI is an independent commission that conducts fact-finding investigations involving criminal and political corruption, the conduct of government officials, and issues in governance. They decide to hold public hearings into the way casinos handle granting credit with the goal of recommending new state laws minimizing the risk that other compulsive gamblers won't follow in Dave's footsteps. The hearings will give Dave a perfect platform to urge the state to boost funding for treating compulsive gambling.

At the beginning of March, the SCI hearings begin. For four days, a series of witnesses, including state law enforcement officials, casino executives, and several gamblers (in addition to Dave) give testimony in one of the ornate hearing rooms in the state house in Trenton. The state officials tell the commission that the casinos' credit practices have led to widespread fraud and deception. The gamblers testify that the casinos' lax credit practices had either created or furthered their gambling problem.

Their comments dominate the state's news headlines. "N.J To Probe Casino Credit", reports United Press International. Dave and his case take center stage once more; when it's his turn to testify, the room is packed. The press benches are full, and people line up early to get one of the 100 seats reserved for spectators. Dave testifies for several hours, discussing the entire trajectory of his gambling "career" at Resorts and Caesars. Near the end of the testimony, the commissioner asks Dave if he felt he was a victim of the casinos.

"During 1980, I believe I was a victim," Dave admits. He goes on to spell out his journey toward the realization that he had no control over his gambling. "It is hard to admit that one is a compulsive gambler," he acknowledges ruefully.

He doesn't heap all the blame onto resorts, however.

"During 1978 and 1979, I don't think Resorts did anything wrong," Dave says. The following year, 1980, was a different matter. "I felt that in the period from January 1 to April 1, 1980, I was gambling absolutely compulsively. My family knew it. My friends knew it. I'm sure the casino knew it."

Nevertheless, Dave adds, he didn't know it himself at the time, and wasn't able to resist incentives offered by Resorts to keep betting monies he couldn't afford to lose.

"I didn't know I was compulsive until I joined Gamblers Anonymous on December 9, 1980."

Dave stops talking for a second, to maintain his composure. He has come to realize, Dave explains when he resumes his testimony, that it's difficult for anyone who isn't battling this illness to understand what it's all about. But he says its reach and spread are vast.

"There are six million people out there that are potential compulsive gamblers. It's devastating."

Dave scans the room full of spectators, then returns his gaze to the Commissioner. "I don't believe that credit should be extended to compulsive gamblers. As I see it now…" Dave stops and looks down at his hands. "… if you would only attend one of those meetings and begin to understand the devastation that exists there, that exists in our society, people coming…"

Dave's voice catches in his throat. He falters, and stops speaking. "Excuse me a minute," he murmurs.

"That's all right, take your time," the commissioner says.

Dave pulls himself together and goes on to describe the trauma compulsive gambling exerts on whole families. "I remember one case in particular where this man said that he had a three-year old child. He was on welfare. He hadn't paid his rent in months… This man takes the child and he goes to one of the New York racetracks, leaves his child alone in the car, and he loses $4,800 in the afternoon."

Once again Dave's voice wavers; after pausing, he continues.

"I acknowledge that the gambler himself has to take responsibility for his actions," he says, finally. "But the casino industry also must bear some of this responsibility. Com-missioner, in answer to your question, yes, in that period, those four months, yes, I believe that I was the victim."

Dave then spells out a number of steps that the state could take to address compulsive gambling, including developing educational programs, assisting the casinos in recognizing compulsive gamblers and developing methods for treatment, setting up treatment facilities, and legislation to fund treatment.

"Commissioner, I'm one of the fortunate few compulsive gamblers who has been able to face up to my gambling problem and overcome it with the help of my family and the professionals who have worked with me," Dave says. He wraps up with a plea for the regulators to take steps to help others like him.

The news story in the Philadelphia Inquirer captures it all in a few pithy words: "Gamblers say easy credit fueled their destructive habits."

By now, Dave and Louise are inured to the media coverage of Dave's gambling. Rather than rehashing the past, both turn their attention and energy to rebuilding their life. With activity on Dave's Atlantic City affordable housing develop-ment projects ramping up, he and Louise start to discuss the possibility of moving there. But now that they don't have access to the Sinatra suite at Resorts, they will have to start by finding a new place to live.

Louise is initially wary.

"It would be a relief for me to leave Elizabeth," she admits. She tells Dave that she feels she can't really trust many of her friends any longer, given the way they gossiped about the Zarins' woes. "I would welcome starting over in Atlantic City," she says. "It would give me a chance to start afresh, find new volunteer work and a new social circle."

Her body language, however, sends a different message. She is tense; her expression guarded. Finally, she voices her worry.

"Dave, I need to know whether Atlantic City is a safe place for you to live." she asks, hesitantly. "Wouldn't being so close to the casinos make gambling feel too tempting for you to resist?"

Louise steels herself for an angry outburst at her suggestion that he wasn't fully in control of his actions; It's how the "old" Dave would have reacted.

This time, however, Dave surprises her by meeting her gaze with a sad smile, and shaking his head. "The idea of going to jail terrifies me," he says quietly. "The thought of gambling and putting myself and our family in that situation again – it makes me sick."

Dave's quiet, heartfelt reassurance surprises Louise. For the first time in over two years she allows herself to hope that they really can start over.

The next month Dave and Louise move permanently to Atlantic City. He closes his Elizabeth office and moves all of his staff to a new office in the small business district of Atlantic City. Dave and Louise rent a two-bedroom apartment on the 21st floor of a large apartment building offering spectacular views of the ocean, the boardwalk, and the bay at the southern edge of the city, bordering the neighboring town of Ventnor. Their new life offers Dave a second chance for his business and the end of his affair with gambling and other women. The move to Atlantic City also allows Louise to build new friendships and to repair their frayed relationship.

Together, the two form an unspoken pact to shelve all the hurt and humiliation Louise has endured because of Dave's gambling and his relationship with Martha.

Dave may have acknowledged that he has no control over his gambling. But when it comes to his real estate ventures, he's as detail-oriented as ever. He resumes his habit of phoning his staff and members of his team of consultants for status reports early on Saturday and keeping tight control over his projects' progress.

Building on the friendships Dave has forged with Pierre Hollingsworth, James Usry and many Atlantic City business and political leaders, Dave and Louise soon find themselves surrounded by a wide circle of friends and acquaintances. As Louise comes out of her shell, she quickly gains a local reputation for her warm hospitality and delicious meals, including her famous Hungarian chicken paprikash and holiday ruggelach. No one turns down an invitation to a Zarin dinner party; Louise's baked brownies are a favorite with members of her bridge club.

Louise begins to take courses in art history at the local college and becomes an active volunteer for the Child Federation of Atlantic City, a clinic providing medical care to uninsured children. Rich, Robin and I are thrilled to see our parents settle into domestic serenity after all the tumult of recent years. We enjoy visiting them, particularly during the summer months when our kids can swim in their apartment complex pool and we can stroll the boardwalk and beach. Despite Dave's "go" schedule and myriad projects in progress, he always makes time to take his visiting grandchildren to ToysRUs and tell them to "pick out anything." Rich's two daughters, ages 9 and 11, tag along with him to the office where he sits them down at a desk and assigns them tasks like answering phones or making photocopies. Although Dave still sometimes loses his temper with Louise, nowadays he quickly catches himself and apologizes. Dave clearly enjoys more "down time" with Louise at home, and we all begin to trust that he's truly a changed man.

In July 1983, the Division of Gaming Enforcement completes its investigation into casino practices in Atlantic City and determines that Resorts violated the law when it extended unlimited credit to Dave. A few weeks later, the Casino Control Commission fines Resorts $130,000 for 13 violations of law regarding how it handled granting credit to its clientele. This is a relatively light penalty and Dave interprets it as a signal that the regulators are eager to put this matter behind them.

But just as Dave begins to believe the aftershocks from his gambling debacle are fading, its ghost rears its head in a new and menacing way. Dave and Louise receive a troubling letter from the Internal Revenue Service notifying them that the agency will be auditing their 1980 income tax returns. "It's no big deal," Dave comforts Louise, trying to reassure himself as much as his wife. He finds a reason for his optimism. "The IRS has been following all the publicity about my gambling and the legal issues, so they want to sniff around, too." Dave could not foresee the drastic impact this review would have on his future.

For now, Dave is preoccupied with keeping his housing projects on track, despite the growing political turmoil in Atlantic City's government. The change in the form of municipal governance (the shift from a five-member commission to an elected mayor and a nine-member council) and the polarizing election in 1982 between Matthews and Usry have made the city's political waters increasingly turbulent. Rather than forge an alliance with the city's African American community, Matthews treats their leaders as implacable political adversaries rather than constituents.

Matthews also brings corruption back to the city, if it had ever left. The FBI has been investigating organized crime throughout New Jersey for years. Everyone knows that Matthews has powerful patrons, many of whom have links to organized crime, so the FBI is closely monitoring Matthews' activities. In the fall of 1983, the FBI runs a sting operation, recording more than 326 conversations between Matthews and his associates. Then, on December 19,

1983, FBI agents raid Matthews' office and remove numerous files and records. The FBI probe dominates the news headlines and exacerbates Atlantic City's reputation for political and regulatory chaos. The upheaval makes it even more difficult for Dave to navigate the complex permitting and financing process for his projects.

In particular, Dave is having trouble winning environmental approvals for his Lighthouse Plaza project in the South Inlet section of the city. This problem preoccupies his mind during what have become daily strolls on the boardwalk. As he mulls over his business challenges, he savors the briny smell of the ocean. These days, he barely registers the growing number of casinos lining the boardwalk – that is, until he passes Resorts' iconic building. Each time he reaches it, he glances up at its white Victorian façade. He surprises himself with the realization that he can hardly remember the layout of the casino floor where he once spent so many hours – and so much money – glued to its craps table.

During one of his daily walks, a tall man in a leather jacket strides up to Dave. "Mr. Zarin, hey Mr. Zarin, have you got a minute?" the stranger calls out to him. Dave doesn't recognize the stranger, but slows his pace. The guy in the leather jacket sidles up to Dave.

"I may be able to help you with your housing projects," the stranger says, lowering his voice to a conspiratorial tone.

Startled, Dave stops in his tracks and turns to face the man.

"Do I know you?" he demands. "What are you talking about?"

The man gives him a small, tight smile.

"I heard through the grapevine that you might be having trouble getting certain approvals for your Lighthouse project," he tells Dave. "Maybe I can help?"

"I don't even know you. So, how do you know about my business?" Dave asks warily. "And what do you mean by 'help'?"

"Well I got connections. I think I can get them to smooth the process for you," the stranger says with a shrug. "For a price."

The stranger is no longer smiling. He gives Dave a piercing look.

"It can be for our mutual benefit."

Dave stares back at him without blinking. "Look, I don't know who you are, or what you are trying to do here, but I want nothing to do with you."

Dave wheels around and quickly walks away.

That evening, he calls me to tell me about the encounter.

"I don't need that kind of help," Dave says, in disgust. "He was such a sketchy character. Maybe I've seen too many cop shows, but I think he could have been wearing a wire. Maybe as part of the Matthews sting operation?"

Dave soon shrugs off the incident and returns his focus to the complex process of getting his Lighthouse Plaza project off the ground. He has obtained the financing, but is struggling to secure HUD's approval for insurance on that financing. The project can't go forward without this approval and the financing deadline is looming in a maddening fashion.

Two days before the project is scheduled to close, Dave gets a call from HUD asking him to come to Washington the next day. Dave and his project manager Ken Smith arrive the next morning. Arriving at HUD headquarters, a staffer escorts them to a large conference room in which they remain the rest of the working day fielding questions about the project from a tag-team of HUD officials who cycle in and out. As the hours tick by, Dave gets more and more unsettled. His partners have invested millions of dollars in this project and it *has* to close the next day or it will fall apart. Everything – including his professional resurrection – is on the line. Finally, around 7 p.m., the whole cadre of HUD officials re-enter the conference room.

"Okay," they tell him. "We'll do it."

Dave and Ken rush to catch a late train back to New Jersey. As the train lurches out of Union Station, Dave pulls out a big cigar, lights up, and takes a long drag. Exhaling slowly, Dave smiles at Ken. As the Maryland countryside flashes by outside his train window, he pictures Louise waiting up and keeping dinner warm for him. He's eager to give her the good news.

***

Mayor Matthews, still under investigation by the FBI, faces a recall effort just 20 months after his election. The recall will not only decide if Matthews is to be removed, but also his replacement. James Usry is the leading candidate and Dave quietly works his connections behind the scenes with Pierre Hollingsworth to support Usry's election.

On March 13, 1984, the voters overwhelmingly approve the recall of Matthews, by a 2 to 1 margin. The Black community comes out in full force to support Usry, and by the same margin, clinch his election as the first Black mayor of Atlantic City. Dave joins throngs of jubilant supporters at Usry's Atlantic Avenue campaign headquarters resounding with cheers, chants and calls for unity. People who have just met embrace, dance, slap and shake hands.

Two weeks later, the U.S. attorney for New Jersey indicts Matthews on federal extortion charges. The federal indictment also accuses the ousted mayor of promising to help organized crime figures in return for money. The indictment underlines Atlantic City's reputation for inept and crooked politicians. But having dedicated so many years to redeveloping Atlantic City, Dave sees the recall election and Matthews' indictment as a positive turning point in Atlantic City's story. With new leader-ship, and a renewed sense of civic pride, he's convinced that the city is finally on the cusp of a genuine resurgence. And Dave is now more determined than ever to do what he can to propel the city forward.

In April, Dave opens the Baltic Family Practice Clinic, a primary care clinic aimed at serving senior citizens, which his company promised to build as part of his Baltic Plaza project. When Dave was indicted, he had to sell his pending Baltic Plaza project, a 168-unit senior citizen housing project, at a steep loss, but he had remained determined to follow through on his original commitment to build and donate the sorely needed 5,000-square-foot clinic to the city.

Louise, who has steadily increased her involvement in local causes, is proud of Dave for keeping that promise.

"There's so much need here, Dave; thank you for making this clinic a reality," Louise tells him over dinner one night. "I know that a lot of the nurses and doctors I volunteer with at the children's hospital really admire you for that. And I do, too."

Louise beams at Dave and reaches out across the table to touch his hand. The gesture reminds Dave how lucky he is and he feels an overwhelming wave of gratitude for Louise's loyalty.

A Who's Who from the city's medical community, as well as Mayor Usry and members of the city council join Dave, Rich and Louise for the ribbon cutting.

"This is a vital addition to the well-being of our community," the new mayor says, thanking Dave for his commitment to Atlantic City.

In May, there's another ribbon-cutting ceremony. This time, it's the long-awaited groundbreaking for the Lighthouse Plaza project. Once again, Mayor Usry and other political leaders attend the ceremony, alongside Dave's partners, Rich, Ken Smith and the head of the National Housing Partnership. My brother Rich plays a leading role in the ceremony. When Rich steps up to the podium, it's to announce the beginning of construction for the first housing project in the South Inlet.

"We know this is an important precedent for other developers who are closely watching the development of this project," Rich tells the crowd. "We're confident that its success will move them to build their own housing projects in this section of Atlantic City."

"Lighthouse Plaza is designed for working people who live in and around Atlantic City, a place they can come home to and relax with their families," Dave announces. "We want people to understand that Lighthouse Plaza is just the first step in the Inlet."

But Dave still can't shake off the after effects of his past as Martha's lawsuit moves forward in federal court. Only a few days later, Dave is seated with Dino and Jon at the front left table in a courtroom in Newark. Martha sits at a front table across the aisle, with her new lawyer, James Cooper of Atlantic City. Dave and Martha studiously avoid looking at each other.

Cooper opens the case, and in his introductory remarks to the jury, calls Dave a "con man" who is trying to use his gambling addiction to avoid reimbursing Martha.

"Zarin induced Mrs. Nemtin to have an affair with him and she lent him large sums of money as he requested it," Cooper argues. "Mrs. Nemtin loved and trusted Zarin only to realize what kind of man he was when he repeatedly refused to repay the monies she claimed he owed."

As Cooper makes his points, Martha nods for emphasis. Across the aisle, Dave is fuming. Dino puts his hand on Dave's shoulder to keep him from reacting; a quiet reminder that his moment will come.

When it's his turn to address the jury, Dino paints a different picture of events. He portrays Dave as a "sick man, a chronic gambler" who "was at the gaming tables for hours on end."

"Mrs. Nemtin is a shrewd lady who got her hooks into the wealthy man", Dino tells them. Martha sought a share of Dave's business as a way to "finish him off when he rejected her idea that he divorce his wife," Dino says. "Mrs. Nemtin knew my client was 'sick' but she continued to loan him money."

Dave swallows hard as he listens to Dino's description of him and of his actions.

Following those dramatic opening statements, the court adjourns to allow lawyers for both sides time to meet to negotiate a settlement. Dave and Martha leave the courtroom without even glancing in each other's direction.

After six hours of haggling, Dave agrees to pay Martha $961,000 over seven years, with a final balloon payment scheduled for 1991. He also agrees to pay her Resorts debt in the settlement amount of $250,000: he will pay $50,000 of that annually, with the first payment due in twenty months.

Dave wryly reflects on the irony. After spending years in legal wrangling and running up thousands of dollars in legal fees, Martha ends up with roughly the same financial settlement her brother Gerry had brokered on his balcony overlooking Biscayne Bay. Although newspapers pick up the settlement (Montreal's English-language daily runs a story underneath the headline, "City woman settles with former lover"), Louise refuses to read any newspaper articles about the topic.

Martha is ambivalent about the settlement. She's still bitter and can't let go of her grievances against Dave, or acknowledge that her own decisions played any role in the crisis.

"I'm relieved it's over," she tells the press, "but I still believe that the release of my collateral so Mr. Zarin could settle his debts with Resorts was improperly handled and put me in a difficult financial situation."

As Martha's resentment continues to smolder, she redirects her energy toward pursuing her civil suit against Jon.

CHAPTER 12: LULL BEFORE THE STORM

By 1984, the flow of casino revenues earmarked for redeveloping Atlantic City has slowed to a trickle. The original Casino Control Act required casinos to devote two percent of their revenues to urban redevelopment, but also allows them to defer these investments for five years. At the end of that period, they can opt to pay a tax rather than use the funds for housing. If the city is to move forward on building affordable housing, it needs a structure that will emphasize direct investment and close that loophole.

Dave lobbies State Senator Gormley hard on this issue. A former Marine, Gormley, a Republican, is in the senate seat Steve Perskie, a Democrat, held before being appointed as a New Jersey superior court judge. Back in the day, Dave and Perskie were partners on efforts to improve Atlantic City housing. Dave has no such relationship with Gormley, and struggles to find common ground.

"He's egotistical and no big fan of housing – unless he can get credit for it," he tells Rich.

Dave lobbies Gormley anyway.

"We need a mechanism that directs some of the casino profits into a housing fund, to be loaned at below market interest rates," he tells the state senator, during one of several meetings to discuss Atlantic City's struggles.

"That's essential to lowering the cost of construction. We also need grants to subsidize project mortgage payments."

"I'll see what can be done," Gormley says, doubtfully.

Gormley's lack of interest doesn't surprise Dave. He knows he needs to hedge his bets by lobbying several other legislators for a new measure. His efforts pay off. When the state legislature votes in December of 1984 to establish the Casino Reinvestment Development Authority, they direct that casinos must contribute 1.25 percent of their annual gross revenues to fund the new agency. The CRDA will then direct casino reinvestment funds to projects in Atlantic City and other areas. This is a big win for Dave's business, which stands to attract backing for his projects, and a win for those working to revitalize Atlantic City.

And yet, Atlantic City's revival remains as elusive as ever. In 1985, nearly nine years after passage of casino gambling, Atlantic City is still a shabby shell of its former self. Beyond the glitzy and profitable casinos, little has changed in the past decade. True, some significant new housing developments have sprouted up, but they're not enough to transform the city into a genuinely livable place for all its residents. Then, the Matthews prosecution only further damages the city's reputation. The city remains deeply divided along racial lines. Mayor Usry's administration struggles to build a consensus among members of a divided City Council,. The belief that legalized gambling would propel Atlantic City into a bright new future is proving to be a myth.

***

In May, 1985, Martha's $5 million lawsuit against Jon comes to trial in federal court in Camden before Judge Stanley Brotman, a highly regarded judge. Jon doesn't have much confidence in the lawyer his insurance carrier has assigned to the case, exacerbating his anxiety and his anger at Martha. The attorney, Richard Amdar, isn't a commercial lawyer and doesn't understand the technicalities involved in creating a security interest in property. The day before the trial, Jon is irate because he believes his lawyer still doesn't understand the case.

"Ah, don't worry," Amdar tells Jon cavalierly. "Just wear a brown suit, wear a watch. You weren't her lawyer. Don't worry about it. You'll be fine."

Jon is incredulous.

"What? I'm going to trial, she's suing me for $5 million, and you're trial preparation is to tell me to wear a brown suit?"

"Don't worry, "Amdar repeats, with a dismissive wave of his hand. "Anyway, I have another case tomorrow before a judge in state court. So I'm sure your case will be postponed."

In a panic, Jon calls Dino and asks him to come to the courthouse and help because his relationship with his lawyer is so strained. He realizes, even if Amdar has forgotten, that a federal court case takes precedence over state court proceedings: Judge Brotman sends a U.S. Marshall to escort Amdar out of the state court and bring him to the federal court room.

As Jon climbs the steps to the courthouse, Jim Cooper, Martha's attorney, is waiting for him.

"Can I talk to you?" asks Cooper.

"Sure," Jon says, moving to one side.

"Look, this is the worst experience I have ever had as a lawyer," Cooper tells him, lowering his voice.

"As I'm sure you know, I have a very difficult client." Cooper goes on to tell Jon that he feels badly about becoming involved in the case, especially after realizing that Jon's new wife is a friend of his own family.

"I didn't really know Martha when I took this case," Cooper adds, looking around him anxiously. "Please, get your insurance company to give us something, anything, to make an offer. Give me something. I'll take it to her."

Jon looks at Cooper directly in the eyes. "Jimmy, thank you for the personal sentiments, but you tell Martha she can go fuck herself."

Jon continues up the steps; he's still angry, but feels sympathy for Cooper.

When Judge Brotman opens deliberations, it is Dino and Cooper who begin arguing in front of the judge's bench as Amdar stands by, mute. As Cooper tries to convince Dino to settle the case, the two advocates' voices grow louder and more heated. Finally, Brotman puts up his hand to compel silence.

"Can I talk to Mr. Epstein alone?" the judge asks.

He excuses the other lawyers, who return to their seats as Jon approaches the bench. Brotman looks at Jon and leans over to talk softly to him.

"Well, I'm sure you did nothing wrong," says the judge, who has never met Jon before. "You know, maybe, you know, you're a young lawyer, and maybe if you had more experience you might have done something differently. But I get it," he says, shooting a sidelong glance at Martha seated a few feet away. He looks back at Jon. "You will face a Camden jury that may not be sympathetic."

"Give her some money," he tells my friend, softly. "That's why you have insurance."

Jon gets the point and nods. The judge declares a recess and Dino settles the case, for $75,000. Another chapter in this long nightmare is finally at an end.

***

Careful to keep a low profile, Dave enlists his wide network to help political candidates who support his vision for Atlantic City housing. When State Senator Gormley is up for re-election, Dave decides instead to support Arlene Grosch, a highly regarded private attorney, specializing in civil rights, labor law and family law, in a challenge to replace Gormley. Dave shows up at Arlene's home, unsolicited, offering whatever help she needs to win. He introduces her to campaign donors and advises her on Atlantic City's politics. Although Gormley wins reelection, the campaign turns Arlene and her husband George, a prominent physician, into lifelong friends for the Zarins.

With the passing years, a sense of contentment and purpose settles over Dave who no longer seems to crave the adrenaline charge he once felt from gambling. The battle to restore Atlantic City to its former glory is enough of a challenge for him. Dave is pleased with the progress of his housing projects as he contends with normal business challenges and cycles. He doesn't take his recovery for granted, however. Dave still attends weekly

Gambler's Anonymous meetings and remains an active fundraiser. He has made numerous trips around the country speaking on behalf of Gamblers Anonymous. He becomes chairman of the advisory board of the National Council for the Study and Treatment of Pathological Gambling. Dave employs his political skills to convince the state legislature to provide an annual grant of $200,000 to the foundation to help compulsive gamblers. Dave also donates $100,000 through the foundation to establish and pay the costs for six patient beds at John Hopkins hospital dedicated to the treatment of compulsive gamblers.

Dave and Louise finally feel safe, relieved that the legal issues are resolved.

But then, a letter arrives. From the IRS.

CHAPTER 13: THE TAXMAN COMETH

The letter comes on April Fool's Day of 1986. But it's far from a joke.

It's about the tax returns Dave and Louise filed for 1980 and 1981.Technically it's referred to as a "Notice of Deficiency," and in it, the IRS asserts that the Zarins failed to report $3,435,000 of income for the tax year 1980. Since Dave's income in 1980 put him in the 70 percent tax bracket, and Dave and Louise are also liable for interest and penalties, the IRS asserts that Dave and Louise now owe a whopping $5 million to the IRS for 1980.

Louise and Dave are shocked. How can the IRS recast $3,435,000 in gambling *losses* as income? To the agency, it's simple: Dave obtained this money through fraud, technically termed larceny by "trick and deception." But the state of New Jersey had already indicted him on the same charges, only to dismiss them and expunge them from Dave's record! I'm shocked that the IRS is serving as a collection agency for the same events.

For his part, Dave sees the IRS claim as a staggering case of overreach. But Louise is beside herself with anxiety. The prospect of owing more than $5 million in taxes terrifies and paralyzes her. Just when their life has stabilized, she feels it being upended, again.

"I thought all this was behind us!" she tells Dave. "We can't afford this – we'll be destitute."

Rather than answer Louise with irritation or anger, Dave understands her alarm. After all the ups and downs of their life together, of course she's afraid, he tells himself. He reassures her with a hug.

"Louise, this case has no legs. The IRS won't win," he says gently.

Louise calms down, but remains deeply troubled.

At this time, I am a junior partner in the Washington, D.C. branch office of a large multinational law firm. My practice specializes in international trade and commercial matters. There are several well-regarded tax partners in our New York office able to handle the case. I introduce Dave to one of the partners, Daniel Portner. He is in his early 40s, very personable and engaging. He becomes the principal lawyer dealing with my father's never-ending saga. Jon and I provide Portner and his two associates with background information on Dave's gambling and help the tax team decipher some of the casino records pertaining to the case. Dave and I feel relieved thinking his case is in competent hands. Just one less thing to keep us up at night.

Or at least that's what we believe.

From the very beginning Portner and his tax team make missteps that eventually create a cascade of complications for Dave's defense. Rather than pay and close out the relatively modest 1981 tax claim, Dave's lawyers file an appeal to the tax court challenging the IRS claims for both tax years 1980 and 1981. In doing so, they open the door for the IRS to assert an alternative and novel tax claim for tax year 1981. They allege that by settling the $3,435,000 gambling debt with Resorts for

$500,000 in 1981, Dave realized taxable income in the amount of $2,935,000 for that year. The IRS bases this new claim on an arcane tax theory known as "cancellation of indebtedness," which refers to the difference between the amount Zarin owed ($3,435,000) to Resorts and the settlement amount ($500,000) he paid. Under this tax theory, if a debt is canceled, forgiven or discharged, the IRS can treat the amount of the canceled debt as taxable income. Apparently concerned about the weakness of its claim of income from larceny by trick and deception, the IRS now asserts an additional tax claim for tax year 1981.

***

Leaving the details of the case to his attorneys to handle, Dave doggedly forges ahead with his vision for Atlantic City revitalization. Nothing, he resolves to himself, will stop him from fulfilling that dream. On May 3, 1987, he breaks ground on the Vermont Plaza project, a 201-unit high-rise with five adjacent two-story buildings. It's his third affordable housing project in the South Inlet. The deal requires complex financing: the money to build Vermont Plaza comes from five different sources and totals nearly $30 million. This is the first project to receive funds from the two percent levy on casino revenues through the new Casino Reinvestment Development Authority (CRDA).

Dave has had to overcome many obstacles to bring the project to this stage. At one point, as the project nears its closing date, a bitter dispute between Dave's building contractor and a representative of the New Jersey Housing Finance Agency threatens to derail his project. Luckily, Dave's ability to defy the odds remains intact. When the contractor terminates the meeting after failing to agree with the agency, Dave hides his briefcase – containing his car keys – before he can leave. When the agitated contractor returns to the conference room in search of his keys, Dave seizes the chance to lobby both sides and gets them to agree.

Dave's vision for the South Inlet is beginning to take shape. Just blocks away another developer is nearing completion on a 32-story luxury condominium. Following Dave's lead, other housing developers are also breaking ground there.

On November 6, 1987, the Greater Atlantic City Chamber of Commerce recognizes Dave as its "Business-man of the Year". Dave, the comeback kid, is feted by local politicians, city officials, community and business leaders at a luncheon held at the Claridge Casino Hotel. Rich, Louise and Dave's entire staff are in attendance. Alfred Cade, the chairman of the Chamber, hails Dave for being the first developer to risk building in the South Inlet area.

"While others in the business community just talked about the revitalization of the Inlet," Cade tells the crowd, "Dave came to town and actually did it."

Dave accepts the award to great applause from the key political, social and business leaders in the city. It's quite a day for a man whose career and reputation were declared dead just a short while ago.

As Dave celebrates his remarkable turnaround, a few months later a ghost from his past appears on his doorstep–literally.

Dave and Louise are hosting Pierre Hollingsworth and his wife Saundra for dinner at their apartment when the doorbell rings. Louise looks at Dave questioningly and Dave looks back at her in surprise. Neither of them are expecting any other guests. Louise goes to the front door and opens it to find Martha facing her. It's been months since anyone has even mentioned her name. But now, there she is, wraith-like, swathed in black and glaring at Louise. Shocked, Louise suppresses a shiver.

"What are you doing here?" Louise asks her in a low voice. "What do you want?"

"I need to talk to Dave," Martha replies curtly.

"What about?" Louise's voice rises.

"Dave is late in his payment to me."

Louise returns Martha's glare.

"Wait here," she tells Martha and closes the door in her face.

Louise turns to catch Dave's eye and motions him to the door. Dave excuses himself to his guests.

"What is it?" he asks Louise, keeping his voice low.

"It's Martha!" Louise hisses. "She wants to talk to you about a late payment. Get rid of her, I don't want her in this apartment," she adds vehemently.

Louise then pastes a broad smile on her face, and returns to the dining table to resume her role as hostess.

Dave steps outside.

"What are you doing here? What do you want?" he asks gruffly.

"You missed a payment," Martha answers. "I want to know when I'm going to get it."

"I know I'm behind," Dave replies. "I'll get it to you before the end of this week." Dave turns to the door, then looks back at Martha.

"Don't ever come here again."

Without another word, Martha turns around and like some apparition in black, walks down the hallway to the elevator.

That is the last time they ever speak to each other.

By this time, Dave's tax team has begun negotiating a settlement with the IRS, but the talks drag on for months and ultimately go nowhere. At the last settlement conference, the IRS advises Dave's tax team that they are dropping their 1980 tax claim of income from larceny by trick and deception; and will rely solely on the alternative claim of income from cancellation of indebtedness for 1981.

The hearing at the U.S. Tax Court takes place on January 13, 1988. After the hearing both parties submit their legal briefs to the court. Buried deep in the brief by Dave's tax team is yet another serious error. Dave's lawyers mistakenly assert, when arguing a technical legal issue unrelated to the gambling or the settlement, that Dave was solvent in 1981.

On May 22, 1989, the U.S. Tax Court issues an opinion in favor of the IRS by a vote of 11-8. The court holds that Dave and Louise had "income" of $2,935,000 from the discharge of gambling indebtedness in 1981, and now owe the government $5.2 million in taxes, interest and penalties. The verdict sends shock waves through our family. Dave's business will never survive if the decision stands. Although I'm a novice in dealing with tax law, it always seemed to me that the IRS claim was based on an absurd theory. How and why did the court make this determination?

My father, Jon and I schedule a conference call with Portner for the next morning to discuss that very question.

Just before the call, Jon shows the judgment to his tax partner down the hall. Reviewing it quickly, the partner looks up and says, "I guess Mr. Zarin wasn't insolvent at the time of the settlement." Jon looks at him, surprised and confused.

"What do you mean?" Jon asks.

"Well, if someone is insolvent, if all of the liabilities exceed the assets at the time of the settlement with Resorts, it is an exception to this provision about the cancellation of a debt," Jon's colleague explains. "There could be no taxable income on a cancelled debt due to insolvency."

"Holy shit!" Jon exclaims as he hurries to join our call.

He interrupts Portner who is explaining the efforts they plan to take to reverse the court's decision. Jon blurts out what he just learned. At first, I don't grasp the significance of the insolvency issue. In fact, I'm even a little annoyed with Jon for interrupting.

"No, listen!," Jon exclaims. "Dave was broke in '81 when he settled with Resorts. That means the IRS has no case, based on the applicable tax law.".

Then it hits me and I feel my stomach drop.

"Are you telling us that if Dave was insolvent at the time he made a settlement with Resorts, his insolvency is an absolute bar, an absolute "can't lose" defense against the claim of income from the cancellation of debt?" I ask, my voice rises in agitation.

"Yes, yes, exactly." Jon says.

"Daniel," I ask, "did we assert the defense of insolvency?"

Silence.

After a long, very long ten seconds, Portner answers.

"No, I don't believe we did."

My jaw drops in shock. I can't close it. It's stuck. My hand clenches the phone in a death grip. The phone discussion becomes background noise as my racing thoughts grapple with a new reality, one I can't get out of my head: My own law firm committed malpractice in representing my father.

A punch to the gut. What the fuck. Holy shit! You can't make this stuff up. No one would believe it. By the time I tune back into the discussion, my father is faxing his 1981 financial statement to Portner who then concedes that Dave *was* indeed insolvent at the time of the settlement with Resorts.

Breaking the awkward silence of lawyers who, for once, are speechless, someone murmurs, "Uh, let's talk again tomorrow…"

I hang up. My mouth is still agape.

When I can speak coherently, I pick up the phone again and call Jon. We exchange the same three words over and over for at least two minutes.

"What the fuck!" "What the fuck!" "What the fuck!"

We decide to speak again the next day, when we have had a chance to absorb the magnitude of the mess and our vocabularies have recovered.

Next, I call Dave. He's mumbling; confused to find himself in a predicament he's powerless to control.

"I don't understand how this could happen," Dave says in a shaking voice. "How can they make such a basic mistake? My business is over. I'll never recover from this."

I spend a lot of time over the weekend conferring with Dave and Jon. Rich sometimes joins these calls. Jon's tax partner also joins us to advise on the next possible steps to take. Dave has a hard time calming down. He simply can't understand how this mistake could have happened. Once again, just as it did in the final stages of his gambling spree, his stomach is acting up. He hasn't slept for several days.

Appealing the court decision will take such a long time that Dave's business will go under before the court hands down its decision. Dave will need to tell his investors about the tax court ruling, and they'll probably stop paying for any further project development. The IRS will soon be able to begin collection procedures on his assets, unless Dave can post a bond of between $5 million and $10 million. He can't afford that. A general sense of doom overhangs the discussions.

Several days later, while I am sitting at my desk reviewing a case file, Portner calls to tell me what he is telling his partners at the law firm. "Just listen to me, but do not respond," he says. He starts with what sounds like a statement he is reading, or has rehearsed carefully. "I recall a telephone conversation with you in which we discuss the 1981 Financial Statement. In this call, we discuss the tax consequences that an insolvency claim could have on an adjustment for basis for your father's other properties. You and I then conclude that we should not raise the insolvency defense." He then hangs up the phone. I never got to say a word.

It's hard to describe my feelings at this point. I'd been struggling to comprehend my tax partner's blunder and how it can be fixed, if at all. I am still too dumbfounded to feel angry. But now my partner tells me he is spreading a bogus story about this situation. I am appalled and stunned.

I call Portner back about an hour later and read him the riot act. "Not only did no such conversation ever take place, but it's impossible to even imagine such a conversation. We would never have made a decision like that without consulting the client, my father. And if you knew my father was insolvent, you would never have stated a contrary position in the brief you prepared for the Tax Court.

"Stop telling that story," I order him. "It's totally false."

We hire a new law firm and request the court reconsider its ruling. Belatedly, we inform the court that Dave was insolvent during the time of the settlement with Resorts, and that this issue was not raised because of the gross negligence of my law firm. The IRS files its objections to the request for reconsideration. That afternoon, Dave's attorney learns that the IRS opposed the request for reconsideration because they didn't believe Dave was insolvent. After all, hadn't Dave's original trial counsel asserted in its brief that Dave *was* solvent?

On September 14, 1989, the U.S. Tax Court denies the request. Dave's tax bill is coming due and he needs to post a bond while he appeals the decision in higher court.

I write a diplomatically worded memorandum to the Executive Committee of my law firm describing the status of the tax litigation involving my father, and telling the Committee that unless a bond is posted in the near future, the IRS will begin collection proceedings on the judgment. I leave it for the Committee to decide if they want to post a bond on my father's behalf.

Dave now needs a new law firm to handle the appeal before the United States Court of Appeals in Philadelphia. Jon recently joined a large Philadelphia-based law firm and recommends that his new law firm handle the appeal. Dave agrees.

I then get a call from my firm's managing partner.

"Don, the Executive Committee has decided not to post a bond for your father. The insurance carrier won't cover this," he tells me. "We also don't believe Portner did anything wrong. I'm sorry. I know you are disappointed."

"I'm much more than disappointed," I retort. "This is wrong. My father's business won't recover from this. And all because of our firm's mistake."

Anger is a funny thing. Everyone has a different threshold. Portner made a mistake, a very, very serious professional mistake. But mistakes are human and can be forgiven. I've made my share during my career. But Portner chose to lie about it, rather than take responsibility. And my law firm, fully aware of that lie, is choosing to rally around him rather than own up to the mistake and help make things right. This is inexcusable. What really fries me is the firm's refusal to post a bond, fully knowing that this will effectively destroy my father's business. For me, that's unconscionable and unforgiveable.

I call my father and tell him about the firm's decision, and recommend that he file a lawsuit against my law firm. We hire a new team of lawyers which eventually files a lawsuit against my law firm, seeking, at Dave's insistence, $100 million in compensatory damages and $750 million in punitive damages.

Now that I've orchestrated a suit against my own firm for $850 million, I decide to leave the firm.

Dave's development of housing projects in Atlantic City comes to a halt. His investors stop financing any of his operations or development efforts. No government agencies or banks will provide any financing. He lays off his staff, again. If a bond had been posted by my law firm, the tax liability would not have had to be added to Dave's financial statement.

On March 16, 1990, Dave's appellate attorneys file an appeal to the United States Court of Appeals for the Third Circuit. The stakes couldn't be higher. We all understand that if Dave loses the appeal, Dave and Louise will be destitute, and will spend the rest of their lives trying to pay back the IRS. You can't even declare bankruptcy to resolve an IRS debt.

The head of the tax department is 54-year-old Bill Goldstein, a Harvard graduate. He's known in the firm as a rainmaker, someone who brings in clients, and is usually too busy to get into the details of each case. Theodore Seto, a junior tax partner, will handle research and writing the brief. This turns out to be a stroke of luck for Dave. Ted, 42 years old, six feet tall, husky and another Harvard graduate, resembles a law professor rather than a high-powered attorney in private law practice. Ted is in his element when he can draw on his academic's mind to read, research and write about tax theory. He's precisely the type of person Dave needs to represent him on Dave's unprecedented case.

Upon learning the names of the three Appellate Court judges who will form the panel, Ted reads every tax opinion each judge had ever written to understand their thinking about tax matters. He then spends the next two months researching and writing the brief our team will submit to the court. When the draft brief is nearly complete, Ted arranges for Goldstein and others on the tax team to discuss how he proposes to argue the case. The meeting takes place in one of the firm's larger conference rooms on the seventh floor of their office headquarters in central Philadelphia.

Ted methodically lays out his approach. "As you know, the three judges on the panel are Cowen, Weis and Stapleton. I've read all of their tax opinions. Based upon my readings, I think we have a good chance of prevailing here," Ted smiles. "Two of the judges, Cowen and Weis, are generally pro-taxpayer. They aren't tax experts; they favor simple arguments put forward in plain language."

Ted looks down at his notes before continuing. "The third judge, Stapleton, is the tax theoretician on the court. He often votes in favor of the government and he'll almost certainly vote against us. We'll need to focus our argument on winning over Judges Cowen and Weiss."

Ted continues to lay out his strategy. "As you know, the issue of Dave's insolvency is not a part of the trial court record, and we therefore can't raise it on appeal. So the best way to convince Cowen and Weis is to focus on the plain language of the Internal Revenue Code and to simplify our arguments. First, in order for a debt to be considered income, it must be undisputed and enforceable. A key argument must be that the Resorts debt was unenforceable since Resorts violated numerous credit regulations. Second, it is a hotly disputed debt, as evidenced by the lawsuit between Zarin and Resorts. For the most part we'll need to stay away from theoretical arguments, and avoid any technical accounting issues like the plague. We don't need them."

Ted's face brightens. "The good news here is that Judge Cowen, before he was elevated to the Court of

Appeals, presided over the lawsuit between Zarin and Resorts in Federal District Court. He knows well that the Resorts debt was hotly disputed."

Goldstein argues his case before the United States Court of Appeals for the Third Circuit on August 20, 1990, at the Federal Courthouse in Philadelphia. To anyone studying the docket, it just looks like a routine tax case. But in time it will become recognized as a landmark proceeding.

Goldstein opens his argument with the crux of his case. "Never have I seen a case such as this one where both the Commissioner of Internal Revenue and the tax court worked so hard to find income where there is none," he declares. Goldstein goes on to highlight that the debt, according to New Jersey law, was unenforceable, so Dave didn't have any indebtedness to be forgiven. Goldstein hews closely to Ted Seto's strategy that simplicity is essential and leaves it up to the DOJ lawyer representing the IRS to argue the finer points of tax law and theory.

On October 10, 1990, the Court of Appeals issues its opinion. By a vote of 2-1, the Court reverses the decision of the tax court, holding that David and Louise realized no income by reason of the settlement with Resorts. As Ted Seto predicted, Judges Cowen and Weis vote in favor of reversal.

It proves to be a Pyrrhic victory. Sure, Dave ultimately wins his case, but his business never recovers. He can't attract investors or obtain financing for any new projects. The business is steadily losing money, yet he refuses to walk away from his real estate dreams. Louise is increasingly anxious about his frame of mind, as well as their finances. Eventually she asks me to talk to Dave about his business.

"I am worried about your Dad," she says. "He doesn't want to admit it, but he just can't continue much longer."

I spend two entire days at Dave's office reviewing the accounts and it's clear that not only Dave but the company's operations can't carry on. I sit down with my father in the apartment and brace myself for an excruciating conversation: In a role reversal, I'm now serving as the senior advisor offering guidance to my father.

"The business is losing an increasing amount of money each month," I tell him bluntly. "And there's little revenue coming in. You just can't keep going like this, Dad."

It pains me to see the defeat in his sloping shoulders; he seems to have aged several years overnight.

Dave straightens in his chair. Fleetingly, I see the confi-dence and swagger of the younger Dave in his posture. Then he slumps back, as my words sink in.

"So…" he says with a sigh.

Neither of us speaks for a long moment.

"So…," I finally answer, "it's time to retire. You've done so much, accomplished a lot more than Atlantic City even deserves. But it's time to shut down your business."

Dave nods in resignation.

The Vermont Plaza project is his final housing project in Atlantic City. He retires in 1992.

In the end, Dave couldn't escape the stickman's hook.

THE END

EPILOGUE

The tax court case, Zarin v. Commissioner of Internal Revenue, becomes a landmark tax case. The case appears in nearly every major introductory tax law casebook, and is taught in most introductory tax law courses in law school.

Dave retires in 1992 at the age of 74. During his career, he built 3,783 units of low and moderate income and senior citizen housing in Pennsylvania, Florida and Atlantic City. He won numerous awards for his projects and his vision. Although Atlantic City's dream of revival never materializes, the city today is dotted with nine well-maintained, affordable housing projects, totaling 1538 units, designed and built by Dave. Surprisingly, Dave learns to enjoy his retirement. He has many close friends and admirers. His grandchildren adore him. He becomes a benefactor to local theaters and the Atlantic City Council of the Arts. Perhaps most importantly, he and Louise appreciate the remaining years of their lives together. Dave never goes back to a casino to gamble; in his later years, he occasionally goes to the racetrack. He passes away in 2005, at the age of 87.

My father's lawsuit against my law firm was dismissed in 1992. The reason, the court said, was because the taxpayer (Dave) ultimately won in the U.S. Third Circuit.

Richard Zarin, my brother, remained president of the management company that he and Dave established. Tragically, he died in 2001 at the age of 62 of pancreatic cancer. He was highly regarded, respected and liked by everyone he worked with. Like our father, he received a number of awards for his work.

Louise Zarin continued her work as a volunteer and board member for the Clinic for the Child Federation of Atlantic City, caring for infants and preschool children. She received an award from the Child Federation for her 21 years of service. She also served on numerous other boards, including the Atlantic City chapter of Brandeis University, the Jewish Federation, Jewish Family Services, and Jewish Older Adult Services. She took countless courses in art history, current events, film, and many other subjects well into her eighties and nineties. When Dave died, she emerged from his shadow and became chair of the Board of Directors of the family housing management company, learning the business and overseeing its operations until her death in 2014 at the age of 96. She was a remarkable woman, loved and admired by all of her family and dozens of friends. She died as the matriarch of a large and loving family.

Martha Nemtin passed away in 2013. To my knowledge, she and Dave never spoke again after her appearance at my parent's door in Atlantic City.

Jon Epstein continued his career in private practice, specializing in real estate and real estate litigation. He served for many years as the managing partner of the Princeton, N.J. office of a large and prestigious Philadelphia-based law firm. He always looked upon his experience serving as Dave's counsel as a trial by fire, stressful and all consuming, but something that shaped him into the successful lawyer he became. He has received a number of awards for his excellence as a lawyer and is now contemplating retirement. Jon and I remain close friends today.

Steven Perskie served as the chief of staff to New Jersey Governor Florio in the early 1990s, and then as the chairman of the New Jersey Casino Control Commission. He was reappointed to the bench as a judge on the superior court of New Jersey where he served from 2001 until 2010. He currently lives in Margate, N.J.

Dino Bliablias continued with his successful career representing a number of high profile clients. He is retired and living in Florida.

Ted Seto left his law firm a year after the conclusion of Dave's case to become a professor of tax law at the Loyola Law School in Los Angeles, California. He remains in that position today.

Pierre Hollingsworth served as President of the local chapter of the NAACP for a total of 24 years, and remained a leader in the Black community in Atlantic City and a passionate advocate of affordable housing until his death in 2007.

James Usry was indicted in January 1990 as part of a wide-ranging probe of influence peddling among government officials in Atlantic City. Usry was also serving at that time as President of the National Conference of Black Mayors. His indictment delivered a body blow to the pride and aspirations of the city's rising Black community. Usry refused to resign and was soundly defeated in his bid for reelection. He pleaded guilty in 1990 to a campaign finance law violation and was sentenced to 60 hours' community service. He died in 1992.

Atlantic City failed to become the vibrant city envisioned by the politicians who worked to pass the casino referendum. Political rivalries within the City Council and racial division in the city made it impossible for the city to forge a consensus on priorities for development, much less an action plan. The State government washed its hands of Atlantic City during the 1980s. While the casinos reaped rich rewards from gamblers such as Dave, the city saw little of that cash benefit the community. The South Inlet, today, remains a work in progress. The idea that casino gambling could become an engine fueling sustainable growth in Atlantic City proved to be a pipe-dream. Casino gambling as a model for economic development failed.

SOURCE NOTES

This true story is a work of creative nonfiction. The events are based on thousands of pages of depositions and testimony from the extensive litigation and ensuing investigations; thousands of pages of legal and project documents; casino records; interviews with more than a dozen key persons still alive today; and numerous newspaper articles published during the relevant time period. Some of the dialogues are direct quotations; in other cases, I reconstructed conversations based on my memories and the recollections of others who participated in or witnessed these interactions. I also relied on literary creativity to imagine conversations and meetings that I believe likely took place, based on my knowledge of the individuals involved and their interactions with each other. In a few instances, I speculated on what may have happened to fill in gaps in the narrative.

Milton Keynes UK
Ingram Content Group UK Ltd.
UKHW042039080724
445206UK00012B/64/J